ORGANISTS & ME

HALF A CENTURY AS AN AGENT FOR MUSICIANS

Phillip Truckenbrod

A HollyGrove Book

Copyright © 2020 Phillip Truckenbrod
For reprint or extensive quotation permission please email
phil@concertartists.com
with the text involved and a description of proposed use.
Short quotations may be used without written permission if author and
book credits are given in the resulting text.
Cover: West end, Chapel of the Most Holy Trinity, Trinity College,
Hartford, Connecticut, Austin Organ op. 2536
Cover Photo by Len Levasseur, used by permission of Trinity College

***To Christopher Houlihan and
to the future of the organ as a major concert instrument
to which he so admirably lends hope.***

The author (left) with Christopher Houlihan in Florida circa 2010.

Table of Contents

Preface i
1 Early Organ Fever 1
2 First Parish First Organist... 7
3 My Defection Over to the Organists............................. 14
4 Newspaper.. 18
5 Canterbury.. 19
6 Religion and the Arts 21
7 Virgil Fox 31
8 Louis Vierne 40
9 Eye of the Beholder 47
10 Organizational Identity Confusion............................... 56
    The Agent as Disciplinarian and Disciplined 59
11 Business Perspectives 63
12 Personalities 68
13 Conventions 72
14 AGO Conventions as Trade Shows 78
15 Competitions for Organ Performance 82
16 Towerhill Recordings 88
17 Out on a Limb 92
18 Why Organists are Unique in the Performance Business 99
19 How to Read an Organist Performer's Bio 101
20 Glancing Back 107
    PAUL BISACCIA (American pianist): 107
    RAGNAR BJöRNSSON (Iceland): 107

BOSTON BRASS (quintet): 108

RAYMOND & ELIZABETH CHENAULT (USA, Georgia): 108

JAMES DAVID CHRISTIE (USA, Massachusetts): 109

PETER RICHARD CONTE (USA, Pennsylvania): 109

NICHOLAS DANBY (England): 110

LYNNE DAVIS (USA, Michigan): 110

ISABELLE DEMERS (Canada, Quebec): 111

ANDREW DEWAR (England): 111

CLIVE DRISKILL-SMITH (England): 111

ETON COLLEGE CHOIR (England): 112

JEAN-LOUIS GIL (France): 112

STEWART WAYNE FOSTER (USA, Florida): 113

ROBERT GLASGOW (USA, Oklahoma): 113

CHRISTOPHER HERRICK (England): 114

MICHAEL HEY (New York): 114

CHRISTOPHER HOULIHAN (USA, Connecticut): 115

DAVID HURD (USA, New York): 116

PAUL JACOBS (USA, Pennsylvania): 117

NICOLAS KYNASTON (England): 118

DOUGLAS LAWRENCE (Australia): 118

JEAN-PIERRE LEGUAY (France): 119

GEORGE McPHEE (Scotland): 119

MICHAEL MURRAY (USA, Ohio): 119

BRUCE NESWICK (USA, Washington): 120

JOHN OBETZ (USA, Missouri) 120

ODILE PIERRE (France): 121

JANE PARKER-SMITH (England): 122

PIERRE PINCEMAILLE (France): 122

THOMAS RICHNER (USA, West Virginia): 122

J. MARCUS RITCHIE (USA, Georgia): 123

McNEIL ROBINSON (USA, Alabama): 123

JOHN ROSE (USA, Georgia): 124

JOHN SCOTT (England): 125

ROBERT EDWARD SMITH (USA, New Jersey): 126

HERNDON SPILLMAN (USA, Louisiana): 127

ERNST-ERICH STENDER (Germany): 127

DANIEL SULLIVAN & HEIDI EMMERT (Wisconsin & Germany): 128

TRINITY COLLEGE CHOIR (Cambridge, England) 128

ROBERT TWYNHAM (USA, Maryland) 129

JOHN WALKER (USA, Pennsylvania) 129

JANE WATTS (England): 130

MARIANNE WEBB (American, Kansas): 130

GILLIAN WEIR (New Zealand, transplanted to England): 131

BRADLEY WELCH (USA, Texas): 131

JOHN SCOTT WHITELY (England, assistant musician York Minster): 132

MALCOLM WILLIAMSON (Australia): 132

21 Flavor of the Scene 134

22 A Note in Parting 137

Appendix 1: Cast of Abbreviated Characters 140

Appendix 2: TAO Interview.. 143

Appendix 3: PTCA Roster and Staff 150

ORGANISTS, regular roster, (with commentary) 150

ORGANISTS, regular roster by virtue of absorption of Howard Ross Agency, (with commentary) 156

ORGANISTS, roster membership by virtue of competition win agreement, (with commentary) 157

NON-ORGANIST or organ-duo Artists, (with commentary) 159

STAFF members of Phillip Truckenbrod Concert Artists between 1967 and 2015, (with commentary) 162

AGO & Related Conventions TREATED AS TRADE SHOWS (with commentary) 164

Appendix 4: Stephen Z. Cook Remembering His Work at PTCA 167

Appendix 5: Kenneth J. Bartschi Recalls His Work With PTCA 171

Appendix 6: Charles A. Miller Recalls His Initial Time With PTCA 173

Appendix 7: A Quotation from Paul Bisaccia's Book "Piano Player: Memoir and Masterclass" 176

Preface

The connotation of "organist" in America's argot must be fairly wide and fairly narrow at the same time. We seem happy to apply the word to someone making music in a bar, or a guy at a console high up in a baseball stadium or hockey rink, or maybe even to a mustachioed man with a monkey, grinding away on a public square with a tip box awaiting contributions. Usually it's probably someone in a small Kansas town accompanying hymns on Sunday morning, maybe a little old woman of grandmotherly mien who then teaches piano lessons to children during the rest of the week. But many people might not appreciate that the title also can refer to serious musicians who can be world-class artists on the concert stage. These are the organists I'd like to tell you about.

Remembering is sometimes almost a social obligation because the passing on of those memories to the next generation creates the glue that turns us from isolated individuals into a community. My primary community as an adult was a relatively small group of people who identified under the banner of "organists." Let me do my best here to remember my role in this community and to pass the story on to the future as one more little brick in the total fabric of the $20^{th}/21^{st}$ century music scene, or at least in the corner of the world of music these organists occupied.

I didn't start out wanting to be an organist, and in fact I never became one at all. My career eased into retirement with me as completely incapable of playing the first note of a hymn as I had been on the first day I heard an organ in church as an infant. But from infant to adult my ears always responded to that organ sound with joy and an appetite for as much more as I could discover. My first solid friends in college were organists, and it was a church school so fortunately there were organists on hand to befriend and learn from. Then seminary and ordination and suddenly organists were my professional colleagues and perhaps what a few thought of as partners in crime.

Through the twists and turns of life and love I somehow fell in with the organists and while technically never one of them, was accepted into the club pretty much as an equal. The struggles and concerns of organists became my struggles and concerns, and the standing and fate of the organ in the wider musical scene became my fixation on the future. Now my turn on that stage is over and I can look back and remember. My hope is that

Preface

this remembering will be of some interest to the young generation of organists, or fans of the organ, who follow and that it may give them some additional sense of their tribal clan and professional context.

When friends heard that I had started to write a couple years into retirement they assumed, reasonably, that I must be writing about my decades of work as an agent for concert organists. Actually I was still too dizzy from those decades to even want to try to remember them. I managed to write a very long book on Christianity, which I started during a two month stay in Venice because my husband got sick of my being bored (bored?, in Venice!) and told me to start writing something. Then we came home and I wrote about my life and our lives, and managed to turn out three or four variations on the same theme. Finally, bored again during a long foreign sojourn, I grew courageous enough to face my demons and this is the result. I hope I've set down a few things which anyone interested in the organ during the second half of the 20th century and the opening decades of the 21st century might find interesting, and that thereby I've contributed a footnote or two to the history of the greatest musical instrument of all time.

[An explanation for a choice I made in writing this: Throughout I've used a masculine/neuter pronoun when referring to people in general. This is not intended as anti-feminist; it's just the way English was taught when I was growing up. Since I'm admitting herein to being a 20th century person now struggling to stay afloat in the 21st century, I may as well skip the agony of trying to match the newfangled and apparently shifting ways English language pronouns are currently evolving. Hopefully this approach will offend fewer people than if I tried to be up-to-date and got it wrong, which would be likely. I did write this originally with lots of his/her and he/she type phrases, and then decided it was too painfully awkward to let them stand. And as for the use of plural pronouns to refer to individuals, which I gather is gaining steam even in some respected publications, please don't expect that level of sophistication (confusion?) herein.]

Cartagena de Indias 2020

1 Early Organ Fever

During the murky days of childhood when those adults who came into focus were mostly either relatives or teachers, I had one adult friend who was neither. She was a grandmotherly sort who lived in a big house near my friend Keith in our small town named Winterset (Iowa), and I was always intrigued by its big front porch with fat square pillars when I rode past it on my bicycle. Then she moved into my own neighborhood, into a house with nearly identical square front porch pillars, and she became a customer on my newspaper delivery route.

Every day I'd climb onto the big front porch to put a copy of *The Des Moines Tribune* behind the screen door, and on Fridays or Saturdays I got to ring the doorbell to collect her subscription fee for the week. This always yielded a bit of conversation. I was a shy boy and hardly comfortable talking with adults, but she always posed a gracious question or two which let me spend a few minutes in what apparently was adult conversation.

At some point my mother was hospitalized for several days, which frightened me considerably because I was either not told what the problem was, or I was too scared and confused to register it in understandable terms. I rang my grandmotherly friend's doorbell to tell her the news because she knew my parents from church. Mostly I just needed an understanding adult to know of the agony I was going through and to thereby share some of the burden, which she did.

Mrs. Whitman was our church organist. I was a classic church mouse, and so she seemed to me to be one of the town's significant authority figures.

Whether she was a very good organist I'm not sure. I formed the image over those years that she had been drafted into ecclesiastical service because she could play the piano and had sufficient keyboard skills to get through three hymns a Sunday, which is about all our little church utilized an organist for in those days. Even so, we were Lutherans which meant a few phrases to be sung in liturgy, and lots of "Amens." Mrs. Whitman even attempted preludes and postludes, although I can't remember whether they were anything more complicated than doodling on the hymn tunes of the day.

Organists & Me

The instrument provided by our church was an old reed organ from someone's home, and the organist had to use her feet not to play pedal notes (there was no pedalboard in any case), but to pump air into the contraption to make the reeds sound. Ultimately enough pity was shown to the organist to induce someone to install a vacuum cleaner engine into the reed organ to provide the air needed for the reeds to vibrate, and leaving the organist herself with a little more breath to concentrate on her fingers.

The unfortunate side effect to this act of charity was the sound of a vacuum cleaner motor in the small brick room all the way through services, except during sermons when the machine could be temporarily turned off. One could always hear the vacuum cleaner motor clearly, but because of it, one could not always hear the organ clearly. Perhaps that was why our small congregation was an abomination to the great Lutheran choral tradition, and we sounded more like timid school children learning a new song. By long tradition my family solved this difficulty by remaining silent during hymns, and I never really learned how to place my voice when I tried to sing—I think I'm a tenor, but who knows for sure!

In due course Mrs. Whitman was succeeded by the wife of my high school band director, another non-organist who could play piano and was thus eminently qualified to be our church organist. I even took about three piano lessons from her, with the intention of switching over to organ myself when I became the proficient pianist I had little doubt I would indeed become. Alas, I didn't have the right stuff to become a keyboard musician (or was it that I didn't have sufficient discipline?).

Why I became enamored of the sound of an organ under these circumstances is a mystery. I gleaned every scrap of pipe organ sound I could from visiting larger churches, usually in Des Moines, through my involvement with our regional Luther League young people's organization. During sermons I would call up segments of my mental collection and play them in my head until it was time for more actual organ sounds to memorize. This became such a habit that I could not tell if I was remembering actual literature (probably Bach, but at least counter-point) or making it up. Maybe I was actually composing organ music in my head during the sermons. And this proclivity was not restricted to church sermons either. For many years of childhood I was the shy boy silently playing Bach (or some derivation thereof) in his brain for hours at a time while the world sped along without me.

While I wasn't up to organist standards, I did have enough of an instinct for music to want to participate in school band. My best friend going into grade school was Bobby with whom I spent hours trying to figure out how a conductor could get music out of a musician by waving a little stick.

Early Organ Fever

We had both just signed up for instrumental lessons at school, and so we experimented with our theory that if the conductor wanted a high note he raised the baton, and if he wanted a lower note the baton would go down, and thus all of that wiggling of the stick somehow created music. I did a lot of conducting with a drum stick without achieving satisfactory results, mostly, I'm sure, because Bobby couldn't yet make notes of any height on his new instrument, a trumpet I think it was. I had avoided the height or depth or width or breadth of notes problem by signing up for lessons as a drummer, and percussion became my musical focus from grade school through Junior and Senior High School band and college orchestra and marching band.

Band was a source of much enjoyment as well as musical education during school days, but it could be a window into vagaries of the human psyche as well. Before eighth grade the high school band found itself short one percussionist, so the director was to choose a middle school drummer to join the high school marching band for football season. My then best friend Douglas and I were chosen as the candidates to try out for this advancement to what seemed like the big leagues. We were asked to demonstrate several cadences and a few basics. I got the nod for displaying greater control, or for whatever reason, and my friend walked away in tears. This made it a pyrrhic victory for me because my friend had been hurt, and also because I, in my adolescent innocence, felt he should have been happy for me. Then when football season started another friend, Keith, a clarinetist in the band, and I were pelted with rotten eggs after an away game and I had to start learning more lessons about life's little wrinkles and foibles.

My fascination with organ music, well played or not, on a decent instrument or not, may have contributed to my wish to become a clergyman. Churches were the only place one could have access to organ music, at least in Iowa in those days, and I never pictured myself much of any place other than churches in the future. I wasn't enough of a musician to think I could master playing the organ myself, so instead I set my sights on becoming a clergyman—and thus ironically delivering sermons like the ones I ignored as a child to hear more organ music from my mental collection.

My first choice of a college was a small denominational school in Waverly where I spent two years before transferring, in a bold, for me, reach for a less confined world, to the University of Iowa. One virtue of the small Lutheran college is that it had a pipe organ and students who were organists. I immediately gravitated to one of these organists as my best college friend, and from him learned a lot about the instrument although in a fragmentary and rather confused way. I was dazzled by the pipes and wind hoses and keyboards in the teaching studio, but went away thinking that water was involved in producing the sound because I had only marginally understood when my friend spoke of the ancient hydraulic organs he had studied about.

The University of Iowa had a nationally recognized organ department but when I transferred there mid-way through my college career I had just moved thereby to a city where the undergraduate student population alone was at least five times larger than that of my hometown. I was a little too overwhelmed to seek out any of the organist students. Instead I concentrated on my chief career interest by majoring at the University's School of Religious Studies, then almost (but not quite) unique among secular American schools. Much later, however, one of my chief agency assistants, Stephen Z. Cook, had his doctorate in organ performance from the University of Iowa, and my connection was finally established, vicariously, with the organ department at Iowa.

Although I didn't know any organ students at Iowa, I did attend recitals by organ faculty members, and so started out on a long career as a member of organ performance audiences. Just out of curiosity, or to torture myself, I'm not sure which, I've since used existing records and memory to calculate the number of hours I've spent from my life's allotment sitting at organ performances. Judging by the usual standard of a forty-hour work week, it turns out I've spent at least one solid year of my work days doing nothing beyond attending organ recitals—over two thousand hours listening to live organ performances. Of course, for most of that time it was a necessary part of my work as I'll go onto explain.

Phillip Truckenbrod as a degree recipient at the University of Iowa

Then seminary where my organ education continued, although still not as part of the official curriculum. It was at Philadelphia Seminary that I learned organists could climb down from the pedestals upon which I tended to place them, and get just as mired in the mud of life as anyone else.

I was by natural inclination part of the "high church" group of seminarians who favored the formalities of liturgical worship, and shunned the bent of many of the then faculty whom we students termed "lower than a snake's belly." Philadelphia hosted several Lutheran parishes with remarkably "high" church profiles even in those benighted days, and scads of Lutheran parishes of the snake's belly aesthetic.

Early Organ Fever

Soon after arrival in town I found myself drawn to one of these high church places which I discovered because a senior seminarian, our seminary organist, was an intern there at the time.

The pastor was from my native Iowa and I'd known him and his wife briefly there. When he arrived to serve his new parish in Philadelphia, the seminary authorities had warned him that this church was "not to become a hothouse for students" with the defective liturgical gene. What business of the seminary this was is an interesting question, but the dour super-Protestants of the faculty and administration were doing their best to protect their vulnerable charges, I suppose.

On my first visit to this local church I was dazzled by everything I saw, and especially the large pipe organ façade, so promising, and so unlike anything I'd seen in Iowa. The seminarian-organist led a group of us through the building, wearing a black cassock with Roman collar, and telling us all the whys and wherefores of the place. I watched him intently as he told us of glories I had only dreamed could be true in a Lutheran church. Evidently I watched him *too* intently.

Back on campus, to make a long story shorter, he decided that I had been flirting with him during the church tour. "Your eyes were begging," he told me. Perhaps, but if so not for him. If my eyes were begging it was for an ecclesiastical way of life I had never dared to hope could become a real option in the sober Lutheran circles I'd inhabited.

He and his roommate were widely known (in student circles) as a couple, although perhaps an odd couple in that Paul, the organist, was slight of build and a little delicate of demeanor. His roommate, however, looked as though he could be useful to the Philadelphia Eagles, and acted that role to a degree. They planned to be called (assigned) to the same parish upon graduation, with Paul as the pastor and his companion as the assistant. I believe this actually worked out for them, although I've always wondered how on earth they managed to navigate the ecclesiastical systems in place to filter out gays and other such undesirables.

Anyway, my freshman year at seminary was spiced up by several visits from the "butch" roommate, seething with anger and being wildly accusatory and threatening. He had become convinced that I was trying to steal his boyfriend, and had come to warn me off of that project.

In point of fact the thought had never crossed my mind. I was not in the slightest attracted to Paul, and had never so much as shaken his hand, but I was smitten by his ability to play the organ so beautifully. Until his accusatory visits to me, I had never exchanged a word with Paul's roommate. Where did all of this friction come from? I guess from roommate conversations which must have been rather fanciful, and from a general seminary atmosphere which was paranoid and always uptight.

Organists & Me

While my personal exchanges with the seminary organist and his roommate had been upsetting, he did give me the gift of one of my best memories from the whole seminary experience. Just before Christmas break each year the students organized a service called Advent Vespers. At my first one I recall sitting in the chapel totally mesmerized as Paul played Bach's "Wachet Auf" as a prelude. I'd never heard organ playing of this level of refinement and accomplishment before, and I was somehow changed forever.

Soon enough I found myself an ordained Lutheran clergyman, set to continue my journey with organists and organs albeit from a new perspective which I soon learned could sometimes actually place me at odds with my longtime allies the organists.

2 First Parish First Organist

I had requested from my new bishop the most urban post available. He was kind enough to honor that request. But in Iowa back then, "urban" often had a meaning which might not have been recognized in other parts of the country.

So I found myself heading to the western part of the state to become pastor of the Lutheran church in Dunlap, a town of about 1,000 (+/-) inhabitants. At least there were stores and houses around me, and I did not have to adjust to one of the many Lutheran churches in the state which, at that point, were surrounded entirely by corn fields.

Actually, the town was rather pleasant, if quaint. We had our own Main Street lined for a couple of blocks on both sides with shops providing anything one really needed to survive. We even had a restaurant which was surprisingly decent.

And the pastor's residence provided to me was on Twelfth Street, so I had a sort of urban sounding mailing address. That did not fool friends from New York who sometimes came to visit—"Just head to the last street in town," one of them told the driver when a group of friends were to stop by for an overnight stay. In truth one could not go more than a few feet from my house and still be in town—across the street was indeed a cornfield pointing to the horizon.

The newly minted Pastor Truckenbrod

For more complicated shopping, or for a movie, or a hospitalization, or whatever other "big city" purpose, the townspeople had to drive, however. The closest town of greater size was Dennison just up the road, and offering perhaps two of everything as opposed to just one of anything at home in Dunlap. Dennison did have a restaurant which was a little better than the adequate one in Dunlap, and I enjoyed many a meal there during those bachelor days when my kitchen in Dunlap went largely unused.

The more helpful destinations, however, were either Omaha or Sioux City. Omaha became a haven for me. I'd spent three years in Philadelphia as a seminarian and much of that time in New York on various occasions. I'd become a city boy by then, but was now back in the small-town Iowa of my childhood and youth. When I'd drive into Omaha in my Roman collar to visit a hospitalized parishioner, I'd afterward go to the men's room and exchange the collar for a necktie. Then I could walk around downtown for a time before heading home. I was then, in a mere necktie, anonymous; free to wander around enjoying the city without anyone laying assumptions or expectations or stereotypes on me. I probably survived this period of my life because Omaha was there, waiting to ignore my presence. Over the years I'd come to need the anonymity cities could provide as much as I needed air to breathe.

My introduction to St. John's Church, my first parish assignment, had been rather startling. Early in my first week I compiled a list of shut-in parishioners and began a program of visiting each of them as early as possible in my new pastorate. New to the game as I was, I did know that Lutherans expected two things from their clergy: to preach at least somewhat decent sermons, and to visit member households, especially those of the sick and infirm, and that these were requirements, not options.

The very first shut-in I visited, was a man who looked to me as though he could get to Sunday services handily if he really wanted to. He delightedly regaled me with stories about my church organist, whom I'd not yet met.

"That new pastor had just as well not even unpack his bags," she reportedly had told whomever would listen before I arrived. "He should just turn around and go back to wherever he came from."

I had not yet met the woman. Yet she implied that she had my number already, and it wasn't going to win the lottery. And she had been so kind as to herald my imminent arrival in town in front of anyone who would listen. The old "shut-in" guy found all of this hilariously amusing. I sat there wondering how he managed to get to Main Street to observe it at all.

This was long before I came to realize that there was, at the time at least, a traditional rivalry in this country's Protestant circles between clergy and church organists. When I came to my second parish in New York, I discovered that the young organist there would station himself on the front steps of the church at any opportunity to complain about how demanding I was (I wanted to institute Easter vigil, which would, indeed, have called for late hours once a year). Mostly the worshippers entering or leaving church were his relatives, so I found myself on the wrong side of the equation.

Later in life I would become an agent for concert performance organists, most of whom had church jobs as well, and would learn how deep this apparent rift between clergy and church organists often was. But by then, I guess, I'd switched sides in the battle; deserted to the enemy, as it were.

In Dunlap the apparent war between the church organist and me was effectively ignored for a few honeymoon weeks. Then, a few Sundays in,

First Parish First Organist

she appeared in my study as I was trying to vest, just a minute or so before she should have started the organ prelude. "Pastor, these hymns you are picking are going to split this church. No one likes them. No one can sing them."

Probably she was saying that *she* should be choosing the hymns instead of me, as indeed was sometimes the case in larger parishes with a professional musician. I've always suspected she was reporting an uprising in favor of "The Old Rugged Cross" which most likely would have been a welcome choice Sunday after Sunday *per omnia secula seculorum*.

But she had also managed to create in me the sense that I had to stop a rebellion before the flames got out of hand. After all, she had noised about town that I would fail, even before I arrived. So this was instinctively perceived by me to be a challenge I should not ignore as I tried to establish some authority in my new role.

She hurried to the organ and I stepped into the chancel to begin the service. It was the parish custom for the pastor to make appropriate announcements just before (or just after, I forget which) the sermon. The organist's words were still burning in my ears and I had not had time to think the matter through carefully. So at announcement time I asked the congregation to let me know directly if anyone had concerns about hymns or any other matters. "Don't hide behind anyone else's skirts," I blurted out in an unnecessary, ill-advised, and perhaps un-pastoral defense of my turf.

Perhaps I did owe her an apology. But I certainly never expected Vesuvius to blow. After the church had cleared following the service, I found the organist, standing supported by her husband, shaking violently, with tears streaming down her face. "How could you do that to me! How could you do that to me, Pastor?"

The organist/clergy war had found new life. I've always suspected she counted the episode as a victory of sorts, despite her tears and aggrieved protests. "See, this new pastor is a bad apple just like I warned you."

In large parishes, and in large cities, I could imagine how the organist/clergy rivalry could spark to fire. The organist was often a professional musician with great musical ability, and possessed of a local following as a performer. The organist was also the choirmaster in many cases, and thus held a power base in the structure of the congregation through the choir. The clergy were in need of a local following, and were often quite good at their craft as well. Who was really drawing people into the pews—were they coming for the music or for the sermons?

I'm told that during the era of the great concert organist Virgil Fox at The Riverside Church in New York, phone calls would come in before a given Sunday to find out if Dr. Fox would be on the organ bench that week, or away performing. That, I can see, might engender a bit of tension between the music department and the clergy.

But my organist and I were in Dunlap, Iowa, not on Riverside Drive. And, to be honest, she was an amateur organist at best; essentially the only one in the congregation with sufficient keyboard skill to be drafted to move from pianist to organist to fill a vacuum (but thankfully this time not to try to contend with a vacuum cleaner motor).

I, on the other hand, was a wet-behind-the-ears guy who had been ordained just several weeks ago, and was floundering around trying to figure out how to serve his first congregation. I may have been, on good days, a passable preacher, but was in no danger of becoming widely renowned for my efforts.

So, why in the world were she and I dancing this dance? Was it really part of an unavoidable, perhaps automatic, tension between organists and clergy? Was it some kind of irony visited from on high to give the gods an occasional amusing moment? Sorry to report I have no answer to this riddle.

Certainly it was true that in many small congregations the "organist" was a passable pianist impressed into service on whatever small organ the parish possessed. This situation usually yielded just an adequate church organist, although upon occasion one of these pianists caught the organ bug and took it further; something which happened to Gillian Weir, who became one of 20th century's most acclaimed concert organists and whom I would later represent as an agent. As I mentioned earlier, I'd grown up in a parish where this adequate-pianist-to-church-organist transfer was the case and where, probably as a result, the hymn singing was an anemic affront to the great Lutheran choral tradition which should have been our heritage. In Dunlap it was a few notches better, but we still sounded like a mediocre school chorus trying to warm up after gym class.

These sorts of small parish musical compromises were so routine in my experience that when I met my future husband I kept asking him, "Are you a *real* organist?" The idea that he could play musical literature such as J.S. Bach, rather than just grind out a few hymns, was utterly fascinating to me. I had left then, finally, my era of warmed over pianists drafted to pretend to be organists. And without yet knowing so, I had entered the era of my own decades-long professional involvement with the pipe organ and professional organists.

And speaking of the instrument itself, that somehow managed to become a tug-of-war between me and the Dunlap organist as well. The instrument in use when I arrived was a small electronic device of no noticeable distinction. I'm not totally sure why the subject of a new organ

First Parish First Organist

arose. Probably a fund had been started and had reached the level at which our organist felt we could better ourselves.

I'd learned enough by then, from college and seminary experience and organist friends, to know that the ideal goal would be a pipe organ. But I was also aware that we had nowhere near enough money to dream in that direction. So off we went on several committee trips to Omaha to see what the piano/organ stores could offer us.

One company was selling something which looked attractive to me because it had a few pipes on top of the console—I don't think they actually spoke. Rather, if I recall correctly, the idea was that they would resonate with the pitches being played and thus, by some sonic miracle, enhance the sound produced by the merely electronic components.

I had just enough knowledge about such things to fail to recognize how ignorant I really was. I did know we were supposed to go for actual pipes if at all possible, so I became an advocate for this particular machine, thinking it must be closer to the ideal than an organ console with no pipes on top.

But it was not the pipes, or even the instrument itself, which sparked the inevitable flair-up of the always ready to explode feud between the organist and me. She, as it turned out, had made up her mind long before the official search began, and her decision had nothing at all to do with which instrument could give us the most genuine sound for the budget within which we had to work.

She had a friend up the road in Dennison who sold electronic organs; well, to be specific, electronic theater organs for home entertainment use (Wurlitzer), not electronic organs intended for church use (Baldwin, or Conn, for example, as was the Omaha instrument with the "pipes"). I had just enough knowledge in these matters to understand the difference, and so the organist and I found ourselves, yet again, on opposite pages. Why she had allowed the committee to investigate organs from Omaha dealers in the first place I don't know, other than it obscured her true intentions a little and was probably meant to relay the message that the ultimate choice had been a community decision.

Now it was no longer a matter of my feeling I should encourage purchase of the console with the little (phony) organ pipes, but of trying to scotch the purchase of an electronic instrument which I really did know was wrong for the parish. And on top of that, I could read the motives of the organist as so obviously not musical, as so obviously merely wanting to patronize her friend, that I issued a report to the congregation heavily coming down on the side of purchasing the organ in Omaha. She, of course, issued her own report to the congregation insisting that it was best from any conceivable point-of-view to purchase the Dennison (Wurlitzer) organ.

Organists & Me

She won. Not really a surprise. I'd been in town only a few months, and she'd been the organist there for years, as well as being a member of one of the primary families of the parish. So I was left to schedule the "dedication" performance of the new organ which I strongly felt was the wrong choice. At least I managed to get the Wurlitzer dealer to pay for the performer at the dedicatory recital, a guy who travelled around the area demonstrating Wurlitzers. We were treated to "The Yellow Rose of Texas" and other such pop material for which this type of organ was designed. Just as well, perhaps, since our organist was not going to use the instrument for anything more ecclesiastically appropriate in any case, aside from a few hymns (preferably "The Old Rugged Cross").

Now, a seemingly infinite number of organ recitals later, and what only seems an infinite number of years of increasing maturity, I might be in a better position to guide a parish through such a decision. And I'm pretty sure I could handle the clergy/organist tension more productively and sensitively than I did fresh out of school. But the fact that there is such a tension still intrigues and mystifies me.

The tension was real. I've observed way too many organists being fired from their church positions for no good, or apparent, reason to believe otherwise. I've worked on both sides of the equation, in effect, and I'm still fairly clueless about the human dynamics at work in this tension. Maybe it was just some kind of weird but cherished ecclesiastical tradition all along. And maybe organists and clergy view their roles differently now, well into the 21st century, and the tension has possibly eased.

Actually, not every interaction between the Dunlap organist and me was a battle, thankfully.

Her sister had died some years ago leaving a young son who had grown up spending summers with his aunt, the organist. By my time in Dunlap he had grown up to be a very likable and pleasant young man. Starved for companionship with anyone close to my age (the town offered very few native candidates—one tended to leave town upon reaching a viable age) I started palling around with the organist's nephew.

Even though by then I'd realized, and gradually accepted, the fact that I was gay, this was not a romance in any sense, of course, with me being the local clergyman. But it offered an occasional chance to go to a movie in Omaha with an appealing companion, and someone to talk with who felt like a peer despite a few years age difference. The closest it got to romantic territory was when he admired some cartoonish paper flowers I'd put in a little vase on my coffee table, and he called them "gay"—so, in other words, not very close at all.

But I did think of him with affection, and once visited the Dunlap cemetery to find his mother's grave, and to pause there in reflection. It was the kind of closeness and affection which frequently come with standard-issue friendships. This friendship probably saved me from early burn-out.

We were once discussing the future in some context or another, and he said, "I see myself coming out of a bar in New York City someday and running into you again." That idea stayed with me for years after, but it was not to be.

Long years later the organist, in a very kind and very much appreciated gesture, contacted me to report the sad news that my friend, her nephew, had died at too early an age, like his mother before him. He left children and a wife behind. It was so sad for me to try to imagine his death, and now he and I would never run into each other accidently in New York.

The organist's nephew joined a long list of people in my life who died before their expected expiration dates. These 'out of sequence' deaths always brought a specific kind of pain. They kept chipping away at *my own* expected future.

3 My Defection Over to the Organists

The major chapter in my God-Business era, and the final one as well, was meeting the person who would be my life's companion and eventual legal husband. This was also the beginning of the organists' agency period I've set out to tell you about, so it becomes a part of the story.

After Dunlap I served an old German parish in the South Bronx of New York City, not far from Yankee Stadium, and squarely in one of the nation's legendary urban ghettos. The organist I inherited there was a son of the parish, a few years younger than me. He, along with most of the remaining congregation, commuted down from Westchester County on Sundays, and otherwise were missing from parish life. It was a combination of circumstances perfectly poised not to work out well, which indeed it did not.

My second organist at St. Matthew's was a friend from college days who lived in Manhattan in a small apartment with two companions—one was his wife, also a friend from some years ago. The other was an ocelot. Visiting the organist in his apartment was therefore an odiferous adventure which meant sitting on the floor of the living room which was empty of any furniture except a pile of blankets upon which the ocelot slept. The cat, about the size of a small Labrador retriever, had free run of the place. I suspect the ocelot's basic job was to protect the organist from his wife. In any case, this guy was the best musician of the church organists with whom I worked but undeniably also the most eccentric.

A neighboring Lutheran church in the South Bronx was set to merge with one of its other neighboring parishes, and I was for some reason running late as I drove to the ceremony. I should have vested and processed down the aisle with the other clergy, but that was already past when I came into the nave, so I settled into a back pew where I had a view of the whole room.

My Defection Over to the Organists

During the liturgy I noticed the back of an attractive red head as I surveyed the scene. After the last hymn the red head appeared in full glory at the organ console, talking with the organist and inspecting the organ's stops.

I started to walk out of the church but suddenly my legs stopped without any authorization on my part, and they took me over to the organ console.

"Are you an organist?" I asked the red-head, displaying my sharp wit, cool demeanor, and most of all my gift for inventive and original pick-up lines.

He had come to the service with another Lutheran pastor, and he turned to this person saying, "Well, aren't you going to introduce us?" Somewhat reluctantly, I think, the other clergyman did as he was bid. So, John and I met in a church—where else could it have been! Where else would each of us be spending enough time for it to happen?

A friend from seminary was due to arrive at my parsonage (Rectory? Manse?) for a visit that day, so I left the church to walk across the street to my parked car, skipping the celebration dinner by now beginning in the church basement.

As I crossed the street, practically indeed walking on air as poetry would have it, I realized with euphoria that my life would never be the same again; that I had met someone who would be a permanent part of my life—but also that I had no way to contact him again.

I turned around and went back to the bottom of the stairs opening into the church basement. John caught my eye and left his table to come over and exchange contact information with me. "You caused quite a stir in that room," he later told me.

I had hoped John would be willing to become the organist at my own church in the South Bronx. I did realize that its old converted theatre organ didn't exert great appeal for one who had serious talent, but offering him the job seemed like a way to keep us together and, what's more, to let us live together under one roof. Our parallel professional careers did begin at the Bronx church, however, when I asked him to give a public organ recital at my church as an added festivity for Reformation Sunday.

This was my first experience as an organ performance producer, and my first step into the field which would constitute my adult career. I promoted the recital in every way I could think of, including putting up posters anywhere in the neighborhood that would accept them. When I got to the neighborhood bar one of the by then rather happy patrons stood up to inform me that his wife also gave organ recitals—yeah, yeah, sure. Getting into the organ performance business was evidently going to bring along its own set of characters and its own brand of hilarity.

15

Organists & Me

Then John took his first big career step as well. He got an invitation to become organist (and sometime later also choirmaster) at one of America's largest and most incredibly beautiful cathedral churches. And this time the pipe organ was BIG and one of the best such instruments in the country. He was powerless not to accept. So I left New York to be with him, and soon thereafter I left the Lutheran ministry. We were now a couple, and couples cannot go in two directions at the same time. I sacrificed for him then, or at least it registered with me as a sacrifice, as he would do so many times for me in the ensuing years.

It may have been another sacrifice when I abandoned my much-loved newspaper career in Newark in order to concentrate full-time on an artists' booking agency I'd been operating on the side, largely for concert organists at the beginning, and certainly inspired by my wanting to help boost John in his fledgling performance career. But on the other hand, maybe it didn't deserve to be rated as sacrificial; maybe it was what my temperament really called for on its own. Anyway, John and I were learning how to fit into each other's lives like pulling on gloves, so who was doing the other a favor at any given point was totally moot.

This agency, which became "Phillip Truckenbrod Concert Artists" (PTCA), had been planned together with a friend, Henry Hunt. He was from the Detroit area, ironically where the agency, after my eventual retirement, came to be headquartered. Henry and his partner were friends with the organ professor Robert Town at Wichita State University where much later Lynne Davis from my agency roster would take up duties as Town's successor. So I was to contribute John as an artist and Henry was to contribute Town as an artist and, bingo, we'd start an agency representing concert organists.

Henry's involvement didn't last very long as it turned out, but I forged ahead despite lacking any previous germane experience and a half century later could retire looking back on what had been a very successful run as an agent for (mainly) performing organists.

Because of my newspaper work and thus my experience with lots of public relations copy and PR men trying to wring ink out of me, we decided to give the agency a double thrust as both a PR firm for the musical arts field as well as a booking agency for musicians. For some reason we felt it would be presumptuous to use our own names (a decision I later had to reverse) so we settled on "Arts Image" as a business name which we thought could cover both aspects.

Henry and I were both acquainted with Richard Torrence, one of the recognized organists' agents at the time, who most prominently represented Virgil Fox and Robert Glasgow, later to be one of my top artists. Torrence did not appreciate our presumptuousness in this move, and he and his circle

My Defection Over to the Organists

sat around mocking us and calling our effort "Arts Mirage." As it turned out, however, he may himself have been the mirage in that his brand of business dealings landed him in Russia for a decades' long exile which finished off his own agency.

Before the agency shed its initial name and went forward as "Phillip Truckenbrod Concert Artists," I even made a stab at going international. John, on an early performance tour in England and Scotland, had met Freddie Symonds, then secretary and later president of The Organ Club and general organ enthusiast *par excellence*. Freddie had hosted us on our second London visit at the apartment he then shared with his first partner. Sometime later one of us, Freddie or me, I'm not sure which, got the idea that he should run an agency in the U.K. under our Arts Image banner. He worked enthusiastically at the idea, and soon was writing to me on his own Arts Image Europe stationery.

I'm not sure the effort ever got much beyond the enthusiasm level in England, but Freddie did introduce me to a number of top British organist performers whom we then toured successfully in the U.S. I made at least one trip to London specifically to try helping Freddie get his agency working. He was by then living with Michael McKenzie and I was scheduled to stay with them. All I can remember is their black cat "Midnight" climbing the floor-to-ceiling curtains and Freddie deciding to vacuum the apartment while I was trying to nap away a severe case of jetlag. I was desperate enough to move to a nearby hotel, and Freddie was gracious (or oblivious) enough not to take offense. Freddie was an absolute captive of anything and everything "organ" (although himself not an organist, a handicap I shared with him) but he could not seem to extend that intoxication into entrepreneurship, although he continued for years to brag about his role with Arts Image.

Later during my not infrequent business trips to London I met an American-in-exile who was trying to get his own agency off the ground, and who gravitated to representing organists. Great Britain, while steeped in organ culture, was a pretty small market to sustain such an agency, so my new friend decided he'd like to link up with me and revive the idea of an agency based on both sides of the Atlantic. The idea wasn't really practical on many levels, as I by then understood, so I exhibited less enthusiasm than did he and eventually the idea faded into the sunset. Then he decided to move on and try the idea out in Australia, or New Zealand, I forget which, and we lost contact. I do, however, remember being courted while the idea was still viable in his mind—the only time in my life I've ever arrived to check in at a hotel to find there was a nice bouquet of fresh flowers awaiting my arrival.

4 Newspaper

I'd moved to Newark knowing that I'd soon need to leave St. Matthew's in the Bronx because I could not keep the post as a commuter, and on a part-time basis, although for a short time it was handled exactly that way. But I had essentially moved to Newark to stay partnered with John, and was now without a job in New Jersey, and for that matter, without any experience working in the secular world since high school.

My first instinct was to apply to the PR office at a local Lutheran college, since that seemed to bridge my past with what I hoped could be my future. John and I visited the campus one evening in preparation for my anticipated application during office hours. But we found a ghostly, eerily empty campus; the school had just closed permanently.

My next step was to make an application at the local newspaper. I had no real credentials to offer except my desire to be a journalist, and I pretty much knew that would not be sufficient. But to my shock, and to my extreme joy and relief, the editor gave me a trial two week employment period as a general assignment reporter.

My first assignment was to gather quotations from people on the streets of New Brunswick where some minor, as I recall, riots had been taking place over the same economic and racial tensions which had recently torn apart Newark and Detroit. Then, on my first Sunday as an actual journalist, there it was—a front page story with my own by-line; under the fold, but tangible and real. And even better, my position was elevated from 'trial period' to being a regular reporter for the seventh largest daily newspaper in the nation.

In these days when all men (including criminal defendants) seemed to be referred to as "Gentleman," I often remember with a smile a bit of journalistic advice my city editor gave me early-on in the form of a question. I had referred to a woman in my story as a "Lady." "How do you know she's a Lady?" the editor asked me, thereby helping me along the road to cleaner and leaner newspaper writing, and to thinking about the implications of words I used.

5 Canterbury

My most exotic assignment for *The Star-Ledger* was to cover a Central Committee meeting of the World Council of Churches (WCC) in Canterbury, England. This meeting was headquartered at the great and ancient cathedral there which carried the nice bonus of yet more organ, and yet more organ music into the bargain.

John and I had been hoping to travel to England but given our income levels at the time the idea amounted to nothing more than having made air reservations once, before coming to our senses and then cancelling them reluctantly. But with this assignment, my flight and hotel would be covered, which cut our expense for such a trip about in half. Naturally I couldn't tell my editors I wanted to bring a friend along, but I got to make my own reservations so it became feasible; even if I'd been married the assignment would not have covered a spouse for the trip.

As it turned out, John was essential to my being able to do the job. Instead of sneaking one past the editors, they are the ones who actually benefitted as John sacrificed most of his time in England to the cause of filing my copy.

This was well before the digital age, so I had lugged along a typewriter upon which I banged out my stories every evening. Then, however, there

World clerics convene in a Gothic setting

By PHILLIP TRUCKENBROD
Star-Ledger Staff Correspondent

CANTERBURY, England— The tower bells of the ancient cathedral in this small town on England's Kentish coast pealed for an hour to herald the opening of the World Council of Churches Central Committee meeting, calling thousands of Christians of various denominations to a service of worship conducted in four languages.

On the eve of a 11-day meeting which could alter the structure of the WCC and shift the direction of the ecumenical movement, Central Committee members were told by the Archbishop of Canterbury to translate their "visions into actions."

The opening services were rich in the incongruities which are themselves symbols of the progress of the ecumenical movement.

It is at the same time surprising and yet a sign of hope to see a Salvation Army band seated on the steps where Thomas Becket was slain, or to contrast the elaborate vestments of elderly bishops with the suits and ties of Protestant churchmen as they march in procession.

The cathedral at Canterbury is a magnificent Gothic structure begun in the 11th Century and serving as the final resting place for some of England's most illustrious sons. Its vaulted arches rang with the hymns of Christians from around the world praying God's bless g on the coming days of deliberations.

There were quiet signs in the cathedral that new directions are in sight for the world church organization which began as predominantly white, Protestant, European and adult.

The procession passed one black face after another before the citizens of a town who have seen very few black faces. Central Committee members later in the week will deal with a voluminous report from a WCC consultation on racism.

NEW TIES

The tall, black miters of Orthodox bishops from Russia and Asia dominated the more casually attired American and European Protestants who seemed to be in the minority. The WCC now counts nearly every Orthodox group in its membership and has established limited but official ties with the Vatican.

A young man wearing an open-necked, pink shirt with its sleeves rolled up rose from his seat amid colorfully vested Anglican bishops to read from the Scripture. The Central Committee has been charged by last year's WCC assembly in Sweden to pay closer attention to the concerns and demands of the young.

The Archbishop of Canterbury, Rt. Rev. Dr. Arthur Michael Ramsey, outlined the challenge of the next several days when he told the delegates, "Our faith in the gospel of Christ is tested by our actions about race and about poverty."

19

was the somewhat herculean problem of how to get the physical copy back to Newark. The newspaper had a connection at TWA (Trans-World Airline, now long gone) so it was determined that I would get my stories on paper, take the paper to TWA in London, then TWA would fly the paper copies to Newark, they would be picked up at Newark airport, driven to the newspaper, then put through the normal editing process just like a story which would have originated in the city room. Needless to say, this removed publication from writing by two or three days minimum.

But there was no way I could make a daily round trip from Canterbury to London and still have time to attend the WCC meetings, which were sensibly scheduled during the working day. The train trip one way alone must have been at least an hour and a half or more, and then there was the Underground to wherever TWA wanted to receive the copy, so the whole process each day needed around four hours absolute minimum assuming no wrinkles along the way. We became something of an English working couple, with me doing the newspaper/church thing in Canterbury and then John joining me in the evening after his London 'job,' although I still had to do my take-home work of hammering out the next day's dispatch. Needless to say John did not get paid for his contribution—but we were young and grateful for this opportunity to see a bit of the world, so we contented ourselves with the few meals and the few off-hours we could manage together.

This method of filing overseas newspaper dispatches must seem almost bizarre to 21st century eyes, but it indeed was a different world back then. At home at my desk in the city room I used to marvel at the miracle of the news coming in with what seemed then to be miraculous speed and efficiency. In a glass-enclosed room in back of the long desk of seated editors was a row of teletype machines always clattering away as they typed out incoming news from the *Associated Press* or other sources onto long scrolls of paper. The editors would periodically go into the teletype room to rip off a section of paper which would then go to the copy desk and eventually down to the composing room to be retyped on the machines which actually set the type for printing.

Occasionally someone collecting these teletype scrolls would rush into the newsroom and shout out a surprising bit of news, as on one late afternoon when we were all shocked to learn that Senator Ted Kennedy had driven off a bridge in Chappaquiddick and his female companion had drowned. It seemed so modern to have this news reach us efficiently, and yet just a few decades later it would all seem so totally outmoded and clunky. Now the clattering old teletypes are probably mostly gone, as are even the linotype machines in the composing room; reporters now set their own type, as it were, just by filing their stories electronically.

6 Religion and Arts

I'd been hired at *The Star-Ledger* as a general assignment reporter and then quickly given a specialty spot as religion writer. But not all that long later my portfolio grew again after I was asked to take on arts reporting and reviewing as the paper's one-person arts staff—music, theater, plastic arts; everything. A terribly big assignment for a not very well prepared young guy, but I was young enough, and confident enough, to take it on with gusto despite lacking any real credentials yet in the arts fields.

My newspaper had not previously ignored the arts, but it might be fair to say it took a rather minimalist and casual approach to them. We were owned by the Newhouse group which also had a large newspaper on Long Island and whose flagship paper in New York City was the *Staten Island Advance*. The *Advance* did have a staff guy covering the arts, Byron Belt, whose columns were available to the Newhouse Syndicate papers and were run by *The Star-Ledger*. The *Ledger* also ran a Sunday column called "Music in Jersey" written by one of the editors, Hank Wallhauser, who was part of a big public relations business on the side.

During my early period at the paper the most I could do to promote the organ was to tip Hank off to upcoming (mostly organ) events I felt were worthy. He never reviewed any as I'd hoped, nor for that matter was I aware that he ever attended any, but at least he did use two or three of his Sunday columns along the way to highlight significant organ events on the Cathedral Concert Series schedule.

Then one day, to my utter surprise, I was summoned into the editor's office and asked a simple question. On the edge of his desk he had placed two tickets to something (Concert? Theater? I can't remember now). His question was somewhat baffling, but direct: "You like to go to concerts (or theater) don't you? Why don't you try reviewing this for us?" Why he assumed I'd be interested in such an assignment is still a curiosity for me, but maybe he knew that I'd made suggestions along the way for Hank's music column.

Before long music, and the arts in general, were part of my portfolio and I'd replaced Hank as the Sunday music columnist. As my by-line proliferated Byron Belt took an interest in my work and we met a number of times in New Jersey and New York, probably because I was the only colleague he had as an arts writer in the Newhouse chain. He later moved to California but still maintained a column for Newhouse on the arts from a national perspective. We've run into each other several times after my newspaper days, but always in places like San Francisco or Houston, never back home in the NYC metro area.

So my name gradually became well known in the New Jersey arts scene from my many by-lines in *The Star-Ledger*. These sometimes were a little slippery, however, due to the vagaries of the type-setting and layout system. I once showed up in the lobby of the McCarter Theater in Princeton to review the current show there when I spotted one of my previous reviews greatly enlarged and posted on the wall—with the by-line of the paper's husband and wife restaurant critics. I presume it was because of confusion in getting out the earliest edition of that particular day and swapping space without completely cleaning it.

Anything generated by one of the Newhouse newspapers, which operated in several states, was available for use by any other paper in the group. I was never aware that anything I wrote appeared anywhere else, but in thinking back the possibility that it may have happened seems intriguing.

There were two large and well-established musical organizations in Newark I suddenly had to write about. I knew almost nothing about either of them, and was pretty naive about the musical fields they represented as well. One was the New Jersey Opera. I had never attended an opera performance in my life at that point, and had not even heard one on recording. Yet this company got a lot of ink from my paper during my tenure, and I was happy and fairly confident writing about them (despite an occasional mistake which showed up in print).

The key to their success with me was that they immediately accepted the responsibility of educating me, and they made it seem like a pleasant friendship. I was invited to lunch at least two or so times a year with both the artistic director and the chief executive, and the conversation was always very helpful for my perspective, overall or specifically about an upcoming production, but never pedantic and never in the slightest condescending or

Religion and Arts

reproachful for any lack of knowledge on my part—they just gently helped me understand.

And to boot, they would send a little something to me at Christmas season—so when the city room would fill up with people bearing big hampers of booze and food for the political writers and the sports guys, there was the lowly arts writer getting a bottle of Chivas Regal as well. The opera valued me, and on human instinct (as well as professional integrity) I valued them in return, an easy lesson in human instincts most likely. These were not only lessons in how to handle a newspaper guy covering one's field, they were basic human relations lessons which I found very useful myself later in promoting performers as their agent.

The value access to the press had for musicians and the eagerness with which these entertainers would offer personal access in order to court the press came as eye-opening experiences to me, who just short months ago had been confined strictly to the audience. Now, in any contact with performers, from the merely up-and-coming to well-established stars, I suddenly had perceived value. For example, one evening after a performance at the Garden State Arts Center (some distance from Newark) Engelbert Humperdinck (the 20th century singer, please, not the 19th century composer) offered me (well, actually coaxed me to accept) a ride back to New York in his limo. I needed to get my own car back to Newark and so had to decline, but I was a little surprised that he would have courted a local newspaper reporter in that way.

Another example came in New York, and so would have been more convenient to accept because we'd taken public transportation into the city. The star American pianist Van Cliburn had been hired to record some promo spots for a New Jersey arts organization, and I was assigned to go into the Big Apple where the recordings would take place to write it up as a story. The legendary performer was quite personable and down-to-earth, which I found usually to be the case with stars who commanded awe from the distance of the audience. John, my future husband, had come along with me into the city. Cliburn invited us to go with him back to his hotel after the recording session, presumably for an extension of the interview. The story does become a little ambiguous at that point, however, because John was young and attractive (I guess we both may have been then, relatively speaking at least) and Cliburn was widely known as having an eye for the boys. After we left the recording session, John and I decided to go right on to Carnegie Hall where we had been given tickets by Cliburn, rather than stopping first at his hotel just across the street. Still, again, it seemed surprising that a star performer of Cliburn's celebrity would be willing make such an effort to court a local newspaper's reporter (even if his motives might be interpreted as a tad mixed).

Organists & Me

In my contacts with similar musical celebrities after leaving the newspaper world I've found myself perceived to be of infinitely less value. An American violinist, then more-or-less on the young side (at least by his own description to the audience that night) comes to mind. One of the young performers in my charge as an agent, Christopher Houlihan, had shared the orchestral soloist spotlight with this guy that evening (and that very sharing of the spotlight seemed to annoy the violinist noticeably) and so I was included in an interview conducted backstage by the local press. The violinist made it abundantly clear that he felt he was wasting his time dealing with us, and that he resented the attention being shared with a mere up-and-coming performer. He perked up enough for the assigned newspaper reporter to avoid his sounding petty in print, but made it clear that the rest of us were wasting his star-studded time.

But back to the New Jersey Opera. In our apartment building at the time lived a single man with lots of money, a love for opera, and a kept-boy. I knew the boy somewhat because we'd often encounter each other on the bus which ran from our building directly into Manhattan. One of my early opera reviews evidently contained a technical error (not my last in print, I'm afraid); I recall it might have involved my having labeled some long and well executed stretch of singing as an "aria" when it should have been termed a "recitative."

Anyway, at the next opera in the season I entered the hall before it filled up and spotted, several rows ahead, Mr. Opera Sugar Daddy and his boy. Unfortunately the boy spotted me and came rushing up the aisle to gloat that I obviously didn't know a thing about opera. He gleefully spelled out my infraction, describing whatever his keeper had told him, which, presumably, now made the boy more of an expert than I. I hadn't known we were competing on that score, but I was pretty surprised that he felt the need to demonstrate his superiority over me, although given his current "employment" maybe I should not have been surprised. While this was not my only in-print mistake, I seldom was called to task in as colorful a way. Mostly it was anonymous work because I was just another face in the audience, and I did put in plenty of effort to be as accurate and non-controversial as possible while still doing justice to my job.

There had to have been plenty of gay guys around me as I traveled these musical circuits, but I never made any personal friends in this milieu, possibly because of the distance created by my being a newspaper critic. When the local opera company brought in the legendary Italian soprano Magda Olivera (out of semi-retirement; actually she had retired the first time in the year I was born) to star in a production, the event pulled in a large contingent of the New York opera audience. The lobby going into the theater looked just like the dance floor of the gay bar I had discovered in

Religion and Arts

Omaha years before: about a quarter acre of trendily dressed, gesticulating, and mostly good looking young men who were not pretending to be closeted. The other music critic in town, from our rival evening newspaper, called attention to this in print with some unvarnished language. I was rather proud of myself for sticking mostly to the music, although I think I did note that the New York opera audience had discovered us for this production.

Opera has continued to play an important part in our lives after *The Star-Ledger*, but now it is strictly for pleasure and totally free of any obligation to know what I'm talking about when I discuss it—although now, ironically, after years of season subscriptions to the Met in New York and seeking out opera in any country we visit, I probably do actually know what I'm talking about.

Theater seemed a lot more relaxed, maybe because in New Jersey at the time it was largely amateur and done for the sheer joy of it, and so theater did yield a few more personal relationships. Newark itself back then didn't have a fully professional (Actors' Equity) theater scene, maybe because we were only about ten miles from the theater district in New York City. But we did have plenty of quasi-professional small theaters which merged a few experienced actors with enthusiastic amateurs. This was a great source of exploration and experience for me, and I learned a good deal about the traditional repertoire (Shakespeare, for example) while making contacts and at the same time giving these small companies a bit of exposure for which they were always in need and very grateful. It felt like a way to make a public contribution to the arts while enjoying myself at the same time. All in all, a pretty nice job to have.

We did have a quasi-professional dinner theater in a suburb, to which I always had two press tickets. The second ticket couldn't be used by John because of some constant cathedral conflict, so my companion for dinner theater was a boy we knew who lived alone in Newark; a really nice kid, and sweet; a friend who was a (straight, I assume) boy but not, alas, a boy-friend (although all of our friends wished he were their boyfriend, and some made attempts in that direction). He knew we were gay, of course, but he never discussed his own romantic life, assuming he had one at that point.

One late night he came to our apartment in Newark without notice. It was atypical behavior for him, and may have indicated he needed to talk to someone he could trust. But we did not learn anything from his visit that night because a house guest of ours (Malcolm Williamson, just on the verge of becoming Master of the Queen's Music to HM Elizabeth II) who had gone to bed early, upon hearing the commotion, jumped out of bed and joined the group, and liking what he saw was not about to go back to bed before the boy left. To our friend, Malcolm was simply a stranger, so the conversation remained totally neutral and impersonal.

Anyway this dinner theater, to which I normally took the cute boy when I reviewed a new production, had a PR woman who decided she would stage an annual awards evening, something like the Oscars or the Emmys. She had organized a group of newspaper critics so that she would have a panel of judges, and my being with the biggest (by far) paper in the state, I was naturally elected the president of this group (it's possible, too, that none of the others were foolish enough to take on such an extra job). Probably this crafty PR woman was setting the stage, as it were, for more bragging rights when awards went to her productions, but she did handle it all with admirable professionalism.

The big awards night arrived, with me slated to announce the winners, but with me mysteriously unwilling to rent formal wear. Why I didn't (actually couldn't) bring myself to dress formally I don't know. It was just one of those times I simply could not get something done; perhaps I was rebelling against the made-up nature of the whole exercise–the dinner theater was going to hand me the results in sealed envelopes, and the dinner theater had tallied the votes of the critics with none of us ever seeing each other's preferences.

So I decided I'd wear a flouncy blue silk-like shirt which in some quarters would have been regarded as high fashion in those days. The PR woman looked stricken when she laid eyes on me, and immediately found a black tie in the props room so that I would, sort of, and just technically, fit into her vision of a black-tie evening. At the podium that evening I was in a theatrical spotlight for the first time and was astonished at how a real spotlight could be absolutely blinding. I tried to look out at the audience from time to time, only to realize that actors and speakers must need to imagine their audience because they may not be able to actually see it. Anyway, we got through the ordeal, and the dinner theater had all kinds of new awards to brag about.

I guess I was a little embarrassed to be underdressed for the occasion, and I guess I should admit to having a little stubborn streak which sometimes manifests itself for no particular rhyme or reason. And I suppose I felt a tad sorry for the PR woman whom I had disappointed, although she got what she set out to get (and more power to her; she was a real professional).

Professional legitimate theater in New Jersey back then was left to a couple of college summer series, to the McCarter Theater at Princeton, and the Paper Mill Playhouse in Millburn, all part of my beat as well.

It was at the Paper Mill that I witnessed the only severe loss of memory by a performer on stage in what has now been a long lifetime of being part of theatrical and opera audiences. The theater had booked a famous actress (a touch past her prime, but still a big enough name to be a draw) as the mother in "Butterflies Are Free." On opening night things went along as expected for a time, and then suddenly the actress froze on stage and stood there in silence for what seemed like a very long time. If I remember correctly her young co-star, who was doing a great job in his role, tried to help by giving his next line, or making up a line to shake things up, but it was futile. Then, as I recall, someone backstage tried whispering the next line to the actress (as well as to the audience in that relatively small room). Still nothing. Then the actress simply turned and walked off stage. The audience waited in hope for a time, before a manager appeared to tell us that the performance was cancelled.

A press conference was called the next day to explain what had happened (one has to give sharp PR folks credit for turning disaster into gold). The official line was that our famous but aging actress was a strict vegetarian with all kinds of sensitivities. Work was being done on the ventilation system in her New York apartment building. Obviously she had been poisoned by something stirred up by this ventilation work. I guess there could have been some possibility of that, but I've never seen another professional actor or singer go silent on stage after that, and I've been part of countless audiences here and abroad.

(One of my organists, well into my agency years, did pretty much the same thing however. He was performing a long work from memory when he suddenly stopped and sat silently at the console for a few seconds. Most organists in such a situation just improvise until the right phrase comes to mind again, but this time the organist got up and left the stage. When he returned, he was carrying the score of the scheduled piece, and started again from the beginning. I'm sure the audience was as embarrassed on his behalf, as was he on his own behalf.)

On the orchestra front I was a little more prepared to be a critic but still hesitant; I feared advertising any ignorance I might have in a public way (and this did happen from time to time I'm embarrassed to admit). The symphony took me up in its care too. After my first written piece, in which I probably had displayed a portion of my ignorance, the music director (Henry Lewis) called and arranged to meet, and he assigned his personal assistant to keep in contact with me, and even to offer rides, etc. should I need them in covering the orchestra. I spent lots of time with her, and I got invitations to Lewis' home (he was married to the mezzo Marilyn Horne then, so their home was big-time classical music celebrity-land).

There were also two ballet companies in the Newark metro area, arch-rivals as you might guess. One of them made contact with me early-on and always went out of its way to be helpful and appreciative. The other ignored me until I wrote a review the director didn't like. Then, they continued to ignore me—instead they went directly to the editor with steam coming out of their ears and begged for him to fire me. You can guess which company was the most enjoyable for me to write about henceforth, and therefore which of the two got the most ink; a reminder that we're all just human in the long run, and if we want acceptable results from even professional relationships human instincts have to be taken into account—another lesson very useful to me later as a musicians' agent.

Most newspaper critics in those days kept away from having to review organ performances as best they could, which of course greatly contributed to the impression that organ was not an important, or maybe even not a legitimate, instrument on the secular musical scene. But the most likely truth was that most of these critics were afraid of the organ because they were fairly ignorant of what made an organ tick and ignorant of its literature as well. Then there was the constant problem of image—organ performances were usually held in churches by necessity, and most critics regarded churches as places of amateur music-making.

I had a big advantage, however—a partner who was an accomplished organist and could answer my questions and catch many of my errors, and who sometimes was able to attend performances with me for on-the-spot evaluations. And he was a generous personality, so I did not have to worry that he would slant any advice against a fellow organist; rather the opposite in fact. If there were any risk at all, it was that John would be protective of a colleague and want him to succeed and for the organ to appear in the best possible light.

I had a good musical ear and a long-standing love of the organ and its music. I also had the advantage by then of having heard most of the current standard performance organ repertoire many times over. But without John I probably would also have been leery about trying to write about the instrument as a critic. There were times when probably John should have had the by-line in print rather than me, and it was certainly access to him and his support of me which allowed me to venture into the treacherous territory of writing organ performance reviews.

And also because of John and his devotion to the organ as a performance instrument through the important concert series at Newark Cathedral, I felt an obligation to help further the cause by including organ performances in *The Star-Ledger's* musical coverage. I tried to include as many organ recitals outside the cathedral series as possible (the orchestra was not yet able to stage events with an organ soloist in Newark in those days). Reviewing recitals of the cathedral series was trickier because of conflict-of-interest concerns, but through my weekly Sunday column on music I was able to give a good deal of advance promotional support and that is usually more helpful to presenters than a review in any case.

As I worked through the concepts of what the paper was contributing by running performance reviews and what I was accomplishing by writing them, I gradually settled on an approach which centered on audience building rather than anything approaching technical analysis. I decided the typical audience member ultimately did not care very much whether a note was missed here or there, but did care whether the concert experience as a whole was enjoyable and the performer delivered it musically. So I came to feel my work to be a contribution to audience building in cooperation with the local presenters. For the few readers who cared about more technical aspects, they had *The New York Times*, although of course the *Times* didn't cover most of the New Jersey events the *Ledger* did even though New York and Newark were only about ten miles apart. When it came to organ performance, then, the newspaper and I functioned more as evangelists than critics.

The Star-Ledger was (and still is) a morning paper but we always made the effort to get reviews into the following day's edition despite the necessary early deadline. In those days this meant trying to meet the deadline by rushing away at the end of concerts to find the nearest pay phone and dictate verbally to someone in the city room who took the dictation and sent it up to the copy desk. Sometimes I even had to knock on a neighboring door and ask if I could use their personal phone—those were gentler and more innocent days than now, alas, and so much so that anyone off the street could walk into our city room unannounced and talk directly to the journalists—don't bother to try that today at any major newspaper.

And once the story was in the hands of the copy desk and the writer was not in the city room for consultation, there was the (usually remote) chance that an alteration could be made which was there to surprise the writer the next morning. Once when I was reviewing the dedicatory recital on a new German tracker action instrument at a small suburban church, someone on the copy desk took it upon himself to insert a whole explanation of mechanical-action pipe organs. Actually, in this particular case that may have worked to my advantage. Someone at the church disagreed with one of my remarks and I wasn't in the mood to get into a big discussion of the point, so I just said that the review had been altered somewhat from my original which was perfectly true, and thus averted a heated discussion on a minor point.

One contribution I was happy to have been able to make to the music scene in New Jersey, therefore, was raising awareness of the organ, and treating it as a legitimate performance instrument in its own right in the public media. When I left the paper I was able to name my own successor and thus to be sure that the organ would still be heavily on the radar of the new arts writer, and would continue to hold a prominent place in the paper's musical coverage. When he moved on himself within a few years, he was replaced with three separate writers and specialization within the arts coverage finally appeared—no longer was one writer expected to cover music, theater, dance, and the plastic arts all in one portfolio. Now the newspaper situation in this country seems to be moving in the opposite direction once again, with arts and music writers simply not replaced at all when they retire. (And after our 2020 experience with the Covid-19 virus pushing many newspapers to their knees, that situation will almost certainly deteriorate further.)

7 Virgil Fox

In my early days as an agent for organists the country's two most prominent names in the field were Virgil Fox and E. Power Biggs. Both were big deals as recording artists on major labels. Fox was a major performer and also organist at the famed Riverside Church in New York. Biggs performed, although I don't recall him as quite so much in evidence as a performer as was Fox, and he was not associated with a major church organist position. Biggs, as I was given to understand it, was married to the daughter of a big executive at CBS Records (maybe it was 'Columbia' back then), which I'm sure did not inhibit his recording career if true. Biggs also had a weekly radio program of organ music on CBS. I was essentially a pre-formed Fox fan however, from the day I bought my first ever LP disk, his "Great Protestant Hymns." Fox also seemed interesting to me as a fellow Midwesterner, hailing from Princeton, Illinois, an area heavily populated with relatives of my own from my father's side.

I don't recall any real sense of rivalry between Fox and Biggs, a much more contained performer and personality than Fox. Some students of Virgil, however, did privately dismiss Biggs as "E. Sower Pigs," probably more as a sign of loyalty to Fox than an actual dismissal of Biggs (although the contrast between the two musical approaches could be pronounced).

John was now organist of the Cathedral of the Sacred Heart in Newark, with Virgil Fox part of the plot line. Prior to a recital at the cathedral, Virgil took John along to his final practice session there. Because he knew John would be thrilled to try out the organ, he asked the priest in charge of music if John could be allowed to return to the cathedral on his own to play the large Schantz instrument. John then got to play it on his own for several hours, not realizing that several of the priests were listening. A few days later John was taking a lesson from Fox when Virgil's phone rang. It was the Newark cathedral choir director calling to find out how he could contact John to make an appointment with him to audition for the organist's job—Virgil simply handed the receiver over to John.

Early in John's cathedral tenure the person who had arranged the Fox performance there, one of the guys who became part of our concert series gang at the cathedral, showed up at the door of our new Newark apartment. He wanted to talk with John whom he had met for the first time after the

Fox recital at Sacred Heart Cathedral. I invited him in and we sat down to await John's return home, and we talked—or for the sake of accuracy maybe I should say "he talked." The afternoon grew into evening and the apartment started to go dark. I decided that instead of getting up to turn on a light, I'd instead stay put just to see how long this monologue could possibly stretch. It grew darker and darker. I can't even remember when John got back, but it may give you a clue to know that we nicknamed our guest "Chatty" (the 'Chatty Cathy' dolls were in vogue at the time), a name which has stuck to him to this day, at least among our cathedral gang. That group, gradually self-assembled from various organ music fans, became a loyal support organization for the concert series and a set of friends who get together in various settings even now when most members are retired from a fascinating array of highly successful careers (or should I be historically correct and say that we did get together before the trauma of 2020?).

I'd met Virgil Fox, very much a larger-than-life character, at his big mansion in Englewood, New Jersey, when I drove over from New York to collect John after a Fox masterclass. "I feel like I already know you," said the big man, loudly, as he came down the hall, with outstretched arms, to greet me. John had been bragging about his new boyfriend and had shown Fox, his trusted teacher, my photo. Fox was one of those characters who actually did merit the description "larger than life," cliché though it was then, as well as now.

Virgil (as everyone called him) and his big Englewood (New Jersey) house, would become familiar and loved territory for us as a young couple. On an early Thanksgiving, maybe even just our second one together, we were invited to dinner with Virgil, and David Snyder his partner, and some of their circle at the mansion. Fox had a large pipe organ in the basement with a grid cut into the living room floor to allow the sound up—an arrangement which always left me a little hesitant to walk into the room over the small-looking grate. He had also installed a large (Olympic sized, I think) pool which one entered over the *porte cochere*. Fox's artistic manger, Richard Torrence, used to quip that if Virgil's performance career ever faltered he could always go into the funeral business offering "burials at sea."

For this Thanksgiving dinner, two of Virgil's more eccentric students, a pair of maiden identical twin sisters, had been assigned to cook the meal and drive it over, and warm and reassemble it in Virgil's kitchen, before joining the table themselves—when they weren't serving. A phone call from the sisters a little before mealtime advised that they would be late; their car had caught on fire *en route*. "Is the turkey okay?" was Virgil's first response into the phone.

Virgil Fox

When everyone was finally seated at table, Virgil unleashed his version of good conversation. "Now, we're going to go around the table and everyone will say where they were when they found out that *Richard Nixon* would be our next president." Virgil, a Midwesterner by birth, was not shy about his identity as a Republican, or for that matter, not shy about much of anything. Me, also a Midwesterner by birth, well, I was by then about as far from being a Republican as it was possible to be. I started to slide under the table, lowering my profile as much as possible and hoping (maybe praying) that I'd be spared the ordeal. Luckily, the chain response was broken and forgotten before it got to me.

The twin sisters who catered Virgil's Thanksgiving dinner became Fox groupies themselves. They were piano teachers with nearly a hundred students between them and had acquired an electronic organ for their home in middle New Jersey (a Rodgers, I'm sure, since Virgil was then performing on a version of that brand especially made for him, which he called "Black Beauty," and which was driven around the country in its own truck for his bookings) and hired Fox to give a number of recitals on it for small groups of their students, neighbors and friends. Virgil, being Virgil, did not play these mini-recitals entirely out of the goodness of his heart. But he may have felt uncomfortable charging an actual fee to his students who were now friends and benefactors. So the "fee" for several of them was always negotiated in non-monetary terms which probably seemed more gentile to the big guy—a new vacuum cleaner once, a new suit for David another time, etc. Ironically, however, the first of these (the "dedication" recital) was given by John because Virgil demanded his full hefty performance fee. The sisters probably could have afforded the going Fox recital fee, but for some reason did not capitulate to him on that one occasion.

The sisters were organists of a sort themselves and at some point had started to bolster their credentials by bragging that they were students of Virgil Fox. Though he had never met the sisters at that point, Virgil somehow caught wind of their bragging (as he somehow managed to hear about almost anything said about him) and tracked them down and called them on it. I imagine their penance was to provide something Virgil needed, maybe just the beginning of the catered meals, but as part of the process he did actually give them a couple of organ lessons in order to turn them into honest women.

These twins became part of the Virgil cult, and from the evidence probably actual friends as well eventually. And they provided some of the outlandish stories which were always circulating around the big guy. One time they were riding with Virgil and David in his big white Cadillac Eldorado convertible when he stopped for gas and they went to the restrooms. Apparently nature's call was quite pressing and the second sister could not wait for the first to finish her time on the toilet. Suddenly they were running back to the Cadillac demanding that Virgil drive off immediately. "Why, what's wrong?" Virgil was reported to have asked in hesitation. "Just go!" they demanded. When car and crew were safely down the road a piece, their story was told. Eleanor had used the sink while her sister occupied the toilet, and the sink had collapsed off the ladies' room wall and was now spewing a jet of water into the room at an alarming rate.

The twin sisters, David, and Virgil were driving down to Williamsburg, Virginia, for a mini-holiday. When they arrived the hotel was at full capacity. Virgil, never shy, picked up the phone which he demanded from the front desk and called David Rockefeller, his patron at the Riverside Church and a force behind the restoration of colonial Williamsburg. "David, honey, we're down here in your town and there's no room in the inn," one can so easily imagine Virgil stating with his normal sense of entitlement. That Virgil's party was then put up in lavish rooms not available to the general public is somehow not much of a surprise, nor is it a surprise that there was no charge at check-out.

Anyone who knew Virgil could pretty much guess how he would phrase things with his deep voice and love of exaggerated emphasis on key words; a sort of verbal underlining which distinguished his speech whether casual or formal. A few of the Torrence crowd tried to take on his mannerisms and distinctive verbal characteristics as if their own, especially one organist who did so on stage as well as off. John saved a postcard Virgil sent to us from Europe and it shows that he wrote much as he spoke: "My dear John and Phil! You were _faithful_ to send the cards and we are following your successes everywhere with the greatest concern and interest!--! What a shame we couldn't meet over here, but we will meet at home and have a _full accounting_!!! We are enjoying a marvelous _change_ and _rest_ and playing all the big organs. Much love, Virgil and David" The address was perfectly conventional in giving our street number and name, but in a typical Virgilism, "_organist_ Sacred Heart Cathedral" was written below "USA" as if to give an address which carried much more weight and made much more sense than a mere street number.

Virgil was generous in his way, but never to be mistaken for a big spender. Eating out with him was always 'Dutch treat,' even on one memorable occasion when the guest was an out-of-town patron who had just paid the full expenses for his performance at Lincoln Center. When eating out was just a simple bite with us after John took a lesson, the waiter was invariably asked to produce a separate check for each couple. When Fox invited the press to his home to preview and promote one of his big New York concerts, he asked for donations to cover the proffered coffee. Addressing the chief music critic of *The New York Times*, Virgil's manager asked if he'd like another cup of coffee. "How much is it going to cost me?" the nation's best known music critic replied.

It was at Virgil's house that I saw, for the first and only time in my life, an actual (evidently) ghost. John and I drove up the long driveway and went over to the kitchen door (it turned out that Virgil and David were still on the way home). In passing the large kitchen windows I saw, quite clearly, a woman inside walking past those windows toward the back door, as though coming to let us in. I can even describe her clothing (rather old-fashioned) and its coloring (blue and gray). It was all very matter-of-fact, and we were surprised when the door was not answered. After Virgil and David arrived we told them of this strange appearance, and they said, "Oh, that's just Mildred. She shows up now and again." That Virgil's house should be haunted seemed almost appropriate in light of every other outsized thing about the man. (David Snyder calls the ghost "Grace" in a recent book, but everyone I know who knew Virgil remembers it as Mildred.)

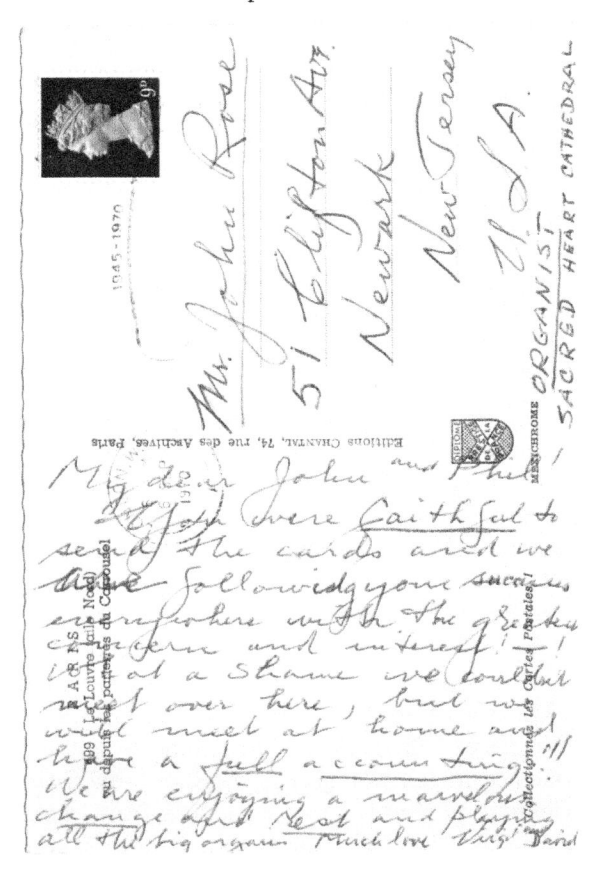

One close friend, upon seeing the ghost himself, was told by Virgil: "Oh, that's just Mildred. She doesn't know she's dead. Sometimes when I come home after a long trip I can hear her dress sweeping through the hall. I just say, 'Hello Mildred honey, I'm home.'"

Fox drove around in an enormous white Cadillac as I've mentioned, the car being as out-sized a vehicle as was its driver an out-sized man. John was always a little sobered when he was Virgil's passenger, and often enough was flung around in a wild U-turn (before the advent of seat belts) when Fox changed his mind about his destination in mid-traffic.

Virgil had also managed to reverse his days and nights, sleeping much of the day and practicing through the night. This made sense because he wanted to train himself to be most alert in the evening hours when performances normally took place. But he lived in the night something like a vampire might, I guess, so if he wanted to contact you in that age of standard wired-to-the-wall telephones, you got a call in the middle of the night. I recall one night especially when he wanted to chew me out for a remark I'd made in the presence of some gossipy queen, and having to stand in the cold at three A.M. "Yes, Virgil"-ing into a telephone receiver in total darkness, still half asleep.

David many years later told me that Virgil almost ended up on my agency roster, although I'm not sure whether that might have been revisionist history or maybe even a false memory by David. I had, indeed, offered to represent him after one of his occasional fights with Torrence. I was hardly surprised when he failed to accept. David later maintained that Virgil was very tempted, however, and had used my invitation as a way to put Torrence back in his place temporarily. David said the reason Virgil did not accept my invitation was that he had already been diagnosed with the cancer which eventually killed him, and did not want to throw that trauma into the workings of a relatively young agency. The timing in that version seems a little off to me but the outline could have been generally true.

Virgil was fatherly to his young students, but in his own way. One aspect he seemed to feel was his right was to know the sexual orientation of the students. John recalls being a late teen sitting next to Virgil on the organ bench at a lesson when the master interrupted a point about fingering: "One, two, three, three, two, one—are you one too?" Most were. Actually, in so far as I ever could observe, all were.

One of my own favorite Virgil moments came as an audience member at then Philharmonic Hall at Lincoln Center (before the organ was stripped out of the hall). He walked to the edge of the stage and said something publicly to Nadine, a blind New York beggar he had somehow befriended, knowing exactly where to look because he had given her the tickets. He then introduced the next work he was going to play, a piece by Alexandre Guilmant. He explained that the composer had played the work for Queen Victoria himself, and concluded with, "So I'll be Guilmant, and you be the queen, and we'll all go to Windsor together." Of course, half the audience broke into loud laughter, while the other half wondered what was going on.

During all of this time Virgil's agent/manager, Richard Torrence, lived and worked in the carriage house of Fox's mansion with his own personal

Virgil Fox

and business partner. That arrangement surely helped with communications, but I always wondered if it put two relatively head-strong personalities, Virgil and Richard Torrence, into an uncomfortable proximity as well. There were frequent rumors of little tiffs between the main house and the carriage house, and a few bigger ones as well. One of the most colorful involved Virgil's partner, David.

Virgil had met David in a reception line after performing somewhere in Canada. According to Virgil's recounting, the younger man had pressed a note on a scrap of paper into the performer's hand while greeting him. This initiated a relationship which lasted until Virgil's death. David's Canadian citizenship, however, seemed always to have been a point of vulnerability back home in New Jersey, and Torrence was not above using that vulnerability during the frequent simmering points of tension. For whatever emotionally complicated set of reasons, Torrence and David became rivals and Torrence ascribed to David the cause of anything he felt Virgil was suffering or any way in which the master's career might be suffering.

At one point when Virgil and David were out of the house on a performance trip for a few days, Richard and some of his friends packed up all of David's belongings remaining in the mansion and shipped them back to Canada. Virgil and David came home to this subtle message, but Torrence and his partner had escaped to California to avoid Virgil's wrath. At any rate, David was not deported back to Canada, even though that had sometimes been suggested as a wonderful idea in conversations among the Torrence partisans.

After John and I began to lose regular contact with Virgil the relationship between him and David took a big business turn when a large "light show" display, operated by David, was added to many Fox performances. By the end of Virgil's life the apparently complicated relationship between the two had manifested itself in David having been legally adopted by Virgil, which I've heard (and seen in the press) yielded another complicated set of relationships between David and Virgil's blood relatives after Virgil's death.

Anyway, Virgil had been instrumental in John becoming a candidate for the organist's position at Newark cathedral. John went to his interview there wearing my suit, safety-pinned down to fit his twenty-year-old frame. He got the job. He was thrilled beyond belief. I knew I could not keep him in the Bronx any longer, where I had hoped he'd become organist at the church I was then serving as Pastor, so I joined him in moving to Newark. The reality, of course, was rather more complicated than that sounds, because it meant I would need to leave my profession, but we kept our family together and that seemed to outweigh any other considerations.

Organists & Me

Newark was in some ways the largest city I'd lived in. Philadelphia was just a student stop, and New York was so extremely large that it was difficult to comprehend, although it had definitely become "home." Newark was pretty much a one-ethnic-group place (at least as perceived in our Italian neighborhood) and its department stores, museums, churches, etc., were contained enough to be understood and managed. It was also exotic in being a genuine mafia town. And it was also the first city where I became a recognizable and prominent figure (through my newspaper work), as did John (through the cathedral and his performance work).

The mafia aspect, came to be felt in many ways without ever being exactly overtly manifest. The restaurants, for example, those wonderful Italian cuisine places which abounded in our neighborhood but which also puzzled us in being largely empty of customers—how did they survive?

We were happy to eat in them with some frequency but it certainly was not our money which sustained them. Father, let's say "Jones," John's immediate boss then at the cathedral often invited us out to dinner, and he knew the best places to eat. He'd usually say something like, "I'll see what's in the Poor Box, and we'll go out tonight." This, sadly, was not just a verbal throw-away line. I was always uneasy to have the poor paying for our dinner, and at a largely empty restaurant, but Father Jones was John's boss so we squelched our consciences and tried to enjoy the ride. The food was always great, and Father Jones was never allowed by the management to pay for his own meals; his Roman collar being the ticket to favored treatment.

John had to play for some of the big mafia funerals in those days, and that always meant city or state police and FBI agents tramping through his organ pipe chambers to keep tabs on just who was showing up below on the cathedral nave floor.

Virgil Fox

Jerseyans On Stage
AN ARTIST WITH THE RIGHT TOUCH

By PHILLIP TRUCKENBROD

The lights burn until 4 or 5 o'clock every morning at a stately Englewood mansion as an internationally respected concert artist prepares his second assault on New York's Philharmonic Hall in less than a month.

Virgil Fox, one of New Jersey's best known musicians, will appear in solo performance at Lincoln Center again on Nov. 25 in the second of a four-part "Fan-Fare for Organ" he is staging there. He is the only organist to appear in solo performance at Philharmonic Hall since the dedication recital series for the hall's pipe organ, and the only organist to present his programs there entirely from memory.

Before the current series began on Oct. 21, Fox had filled the giant hall 12 times since its dedication.

Two hundred people were standing in line at the Philharmonic Hall ticket windows when the last ticket was sold for the opening night of the Fan-Fare series.

When the Englewood virtuoso walked onto the stage, crusty back-stage crewmen who thought they had seen everything were amazed to see most of the full house leap to its feet in a spontaneous standing ovation before the maestro had played one note.

Then Fox sat down to the four manual console and proceeded to play from memory the Bach Preludes and Fugues in A minor, B minor, C minor, D minor, E minor, F major, and G minor. The opening program, appropriately enough, was called "The Bach Gamut".

His audience roared with delight, but Fox, somewhat cocky after completing the staggering program, made them beg for his first encore. They begged with choruses of "bravos" and made him give them three more encores after the first.

Fox is not universally popular with his fellow organists. Perhaps part of the reason is simply that organ recitals generally draw only small audiences and mild enthusiasm, and Fox may be resented for being one of the biggest box office successes in the world of musical performance.

But part of the reason also is a difference of opinion about the degree of expressiveness which should be employed when the organ is played. Fox is famous for taking complete control of the instrument and milking it for a widely different variation of sounds. Many other organists prefer one or two basic sounds and very little variation in volume.

Fox himself defends his colorful playing by saying the organ was not meant to be used "like a typewriter — that just reproduces notes and doesn't add the poetry which comes from the musician's soul."

Practicing for the series is being done on the 52-rank pipe organ in Fox's large Englewood home. The artist's usual pattern is to begin about 4 p.m. and then break for his only meal of the day about 8 p.m. The meal is usually taken in Manhattan, after which Fox drives back to Englewood to practice well into the morning.

＊ ＊ ＊

When Fox is not on the road he schedules about 70 concerts a year in the United States and Canada) his recreation time is spent working on his house organ. He is currently in the process of enlarging it to 80 ranks by adding pipes purchased earlier this year from Boston's historic Old South Church.

As if the full pipe organ is not enough to make the Englewood home unique, Fox's three-story mansion also boasts a full Olympic size indoor swimming pool. Lining the walls and filling the tables are mementos and works of art testifying to his association with the rich, the talented and the famous over his long career.

Like many artistic personalities, Fox has acquired a certain reputation for eccentricity and he is impish enough to thoroughly enjoy acting the part to his public. Many people who have never attended an organ recital have heard stories about Fox dressed in his beret and bullfighter's cape.

But there is a side to the man which is missed by his public image.

On the opening night of the series, when hundreds of people waiting to pay $7 per ticket were turned away, several poorly dressed and groomed individuals, some with obvious deformities, quietly took their places in some of Philharmonic Hall's best seats.

Fox maintains a genuine friendship with many of New York's street beggars and other unfortunates. At his concerts, he regularly sets aside a block of seats to be given free to these people, some of whom have now become knowlegable fans of classical organ music.

Virgil Fox, Englewood organist, practicing at the console of Philharmonic Hall's pipe organ

ESSEX OPERA THEATER
Donald Gage, Artistic Director
PRESENTS

Opera Gala

8 Louis Vierne

A seminal event for the American organ scene began life in a small log cabin in the New Jersey woods which John and I owned for several years during his tenure as cathedral musician in Newark.

Tony and Rollin, our best couple friends were visiting from New York during the early summer of 1976, and naturally we talked about organ. *Of course* we talked about organ: John and Rollin were themselves performance caliber organists; Rollin Smith was a doctoral candidate and historian in the field; John held a major post as an organist and had a recital career going strongly; Tony Baglivi, while like me not an organist himself, was advertising manager (later editor) of the official AGO journal and as fascinated by the instrument and its lore as anyone else who could have been found in the country; and I was running an agency for organist performers which, though young (about nine years from raw beginning efforts), was already a factor in the organ performance scene. I was learning to be a nut case about the organ too, but I was the junior partner on that score in this otherwise hardcore group.

Rollin and John both performed a good deal of French symphonic (sometimes termed "romantic") school literature and were deeply interested in and sympathetic to that sector of organ literature. But they found themselves running against the grain of some of their peers a bit, in that the dominant attitude of the time favored a pre-Bach and Baroque focus on literature and instruments. John had been converted to the minority because of the French symphonic leaning of his primary teacher, Virgil Fox, and because when he arrived at Newark Cathedral he was face-to-face with an instrument and acoustical setting which were well suited for, and almost demanded, the symphonic approach.

Louis Vierne

Out in the rest of the country the trend was certainly favoring composers of the Germanic, and preferably very old (pre-Bach), schools of composition and the minimalist tracker-action instruments people thought were authentic to that literature. It wasn't just a matter of musical preference. It had become almost a religion, with Buxtehude as the patron saint. A whole era of later organ literature, history, and organ building had become quasi-heresy. And heretics like Rollin and John were routinely excoriated, in some quarters, for their apostasy.

Once when John had just performed somewhere in the south, a local newspaper critic approached the local AGO dean at the reception to ask about this strange French romantic era music he was hearing for the first time. Where did this come from and why haven't I heard anything like it before sort of questions were posed. The dean's reply dismissed the whole matter with the back of her hand: "As far as I'm concerned, music like that should not even be performed."

I've always felt that a big part of the reason for attitudes such as that was that performing symphonic school literature is difficult and takes a pretty accomplished organist to pull off convincingly. Certain teaching styles of the day, and their very loud advocates, simply were not equipping young organists to be able to venture into this literature. It wasn't so much that many organists of the day *didn't* perform this music, it was more to the point that they *couldn't,* at least with any authenticity or stylistic grace. They were more concerned with matters of enormous gravity such as whether thumbs should ever be used while pressing the keys.

Much later, after our Vierne festival had melted some of the ice, Vierne's compositions (usually individual movements of one of the symphonies) started to turn up on quite a few recital programs. The cringeworthy way these were often performed in the early stages of revival seemed to vindicate my assessment that a lot of the reason they had been avoided for so long was simply that they were difficult to perform—especially by folks indoctrinated into the tracker-only religion.

So anyway the four of us sat outside our log cabin in the late spring/early summer glory of country-side New Jersey, admiring the blooms on shrubbery I'd planted in the cabin's clearing, leery of the occasional snake we saw, and we did what came naturally—we talked organ (with maybe just a touch of other talk thrown into the mix from time to time because we were all still in our twenties—well technically, I, the senior citizen of the group, might have been a smidge beyond at that point but don't ruin my fantasies).

This time, however, instead of just lamenting the lack of appreciation for the organ's symphonic school, for some unremembered reason we decided to do something about it: we would stage an event which would highlight the six organ "symphonies" (five or six movement major compositions each) of the legendary blind French organist/composer Louis Vierne. Probably the biggest factor in this decision was that we now had available to us an excellent setting in America, the large Schantz organ (approximately 150 ranks) set in the remarkably European-like cathedral acoustics (and architectural beauty) of Sacred Heart Cathedral in Newark.

Rollin and John each had one Vierne symphony solidly under their belts and programmed it routinely; John the third symphony and Rollin the second. Each also felt a special affinity with another, the sixth for Rollin and the fourth for John, and performed them occasionally. That left the first and the fifth symphonies, and we all knew exactly who could handle those exquisitely: Prof. Robert Glasgow of the University of Michigan. So it was decided that the following season of the Newark Cathedral Concert Series would begin with a Vierne festival at which all six of his organ symphonies would be performed in one concert; something which to our knowledge had never happened before, at least in this country, although Rollin had performed all six in 1970 in a series of several recitals at St. Thomas Church (Fifth Avenue) in New York during the Vierne centenary year.

We got busy putting the details in place. Donors, mostly past cathedral concert series supporters, were solicited. John arranged for some choir parents who were in the food business to offer meals for sale at intermission. I maintained that some kind of program booklet would be necessary to tie the project together, and that became my primary assignment.

Everything about the Newark Cathedral Concert Series was accomplished by volunteers, and a couple of days before the Vierne festival the clergy were amazed to see their music director and his friends, including the distinguished Professor of Organ from Michigan, out on the cathedral plaza sweeping up pigeon droppings, clipping the grass on hands and knees, and otherwise making sure the sometimes fairly relaxed standard cathedral maintenance would not embarrass us on Vierne night.

We indeed were *not* embarrassed on Vierne night. The event was a huge success from any vantage point, with hundreds of people crossing the Hudson River to attend, headed from New York to Newark instead of the opposite direction as was normally the case. We even had a phone call from fans in the Midwest saying their flight was delayed and could we please postpone the concert until they could get there (impossible to do, but the intensity of interest was encouraging). Rollin, John, and Bob Glasgow came through with flying colors and the event spoke quality on the artistic as well as the organizational level.

Louis Vierne

I was proud of our program booklet which not only spelled out the various symphony movements and their sequence of performance, but carried letters of welcome from the Governor, the Archbishop, our congressman (Peter Rodino of the later Nixon impeachment investigation), and the current national AGO president, Roberta Bitgood (sometimes nicknamed "Nota" by ever-present AGO scolds, as in Not-a-bit-good—I don't think this was a judgement on the woman, but more likely a way for some guys to show off how clever they could be).

The heart of the program booklet, and one of the significant contributions of the festival to the evolution in organ historical awareness, was a lengthy essay by Scott Cantrell on Vierne's life and work. Cantrell is one of only two major American newspaper critics I'm aware of who was himself an organist and who could write with clarity and authority about the organ for the general public. I'm used to thinking of him as the big newspaper critic from Kansas City, or later from Dallas. When I looked at one of my precious remaining copies of the Vierne program booklet in writing this, I was surprised to note that at the time he wrote this short masterpiece for us he had not yet started his newspaper career, but was still a freelance writer. The booklet also carried a number of photos of the cathedral we had commissioned from a then prominent New York photographer.

After the concert we had a houseful of out-of-town guests and the chaos reached well into the night. I remember needing to go out into our yard under a tree to cry alone for several minutes—tears of sheer exhaustion, tears of joy for the event having been so successful, tears of confusion about how to proceed now that we had under our belts what had turned out to have been a major event in 20th century American organ history.

My indelible memory from the next morning is climbing up to the third floor to bring coffee to Bob Glasgow, and to catch not one but two impishly smiling faces poking out from under the blankets—celebrating the after-glow of an event which was a major landmark for all of us.

Organists & Me

That Vierne festival was a turning point for the American organ scene, and it spawned henceforth lots of smaller imitations and lots of recital programs containing works by Louis Vierne, works that previously would have been considered off-limits by the tracker and Baroque-only addicted organists of the time. The venture gave courage to many closeted organists who no longer had to hide their love and admiration for a giant among composers for the organ, or for the symphonic literature and instruments representing his style.

Fast forward into the 21st century. The biggest echo of the historic Newark Vierne concert came at the hands (and feet) of a young man who had not even been born at the time of the Newark event. John's prize organ student at Trinity College, the superb Christopher Houlihan, (who was also in my judgement was one of the greatest gifts my agency had given to the American organ performance scene) staged "Vierne2012."

This remarkable series of events saw "Houli" performing all six Vierne organ symphonies himself, and in six major North American cities during one summer: in New York (on the 75th anniversary of Louis Vierne's death), Denver, Chicago, Los Angeles, Montreal, and Dallas. Two of these events consisted of all six symphonies being performed in one day, a remarkable achievement with no known precedent. The program in the other four cities had to be divided between two evenings because of restrictions on the total time span for the concerts.

The second Vierne marathon program booklet was a bit more colorful than the first.

Houli had already commercially recorded some Vierne, the second complete symphony, and he performed that completely from memory during 'Vierne2012' (although he later performed almost everything from memory, he was still quite young at this point and the stakes were high, so he had music on the rack for the other five symphonies although just as a safety back-up for the mostly memorized balance).

My link to this high profile series of performances, aside from then representing Christopher as his agent, was again the program booklet. This time advances in printing, or at least reductions in printing costs, allowed glossy, heavy, paper and full color photos. The essay on Vierne this time was my work, although obviously leaning heavily on Scott Cantrell's 20th century original but carefully avoiding copyright violation, and significantly shorter. Houli himself, versatile as he is, wrote the extensive program notes. My colleague Ray Albright did the heavy lifting of organizing and supervising the composition, layout and printing of the booklet. Many of

Louis Vierne

the photos and much research help came from Rollin Smith, another tie to the Newark festival.

Houli by then was showing his gifts as the pied piper he became, and his magnetism drew all kinds of other help and financial contributions into the project, one of which was a fully professional promotional video contributed by an expensive New York video house, a performance of the Vierne sixth organ symphony Final movement, which is still available on 'YouTube' and continues to draw viewers.

Once again, this endeavor spawned lots of imitation, which I guess, as they say, is the most sincere form of flattery. And again it supercharged interest in Vierne and his music, although this time they were not in a deep decline as they had been before the Newark festival. Since then another notable Vierne anniversary has arrived, and I note from TAO that among performance events it has triggered is another one-performer series offering the six symphonies, only this time spread out over several days rather than in a single evening.

Press reaction to Christopher's 'Vierne2012' often expressed a "where has this music been" sort of surprise. *The Los Angeles Times* called the event "a major surprise of the summer, a true revelation." It went on to describe an "unnervingly honest and direct performance astonishing for so young a performer. The Houli Fans can give themselves high fives. They've helped launch a major career."

Christopher Houlihan began his 2012 Vierne marathon performances on the exact seventy-fifth anniversary of Vierne's death on the organ bench at Notre Dame.

The Wall Street Journal called them "Dazzling performances displaying a virtuoso's technical prowess, an architect's grasp of structure and a torch singer's ability to convey emotions." *The New York Times* echoed that "The gifted young organist Christopher Houlihan phrased with flexibility and clarity through the works' knottiest chromatic wanderings" and that "his playing had a glamorous sheen."

Organists & Me

"Houlihan showed great virtuosity as well as ingenuity" and "played with great expressive restraint and elegance...a virtuosic reading," said the *Chicago Classical Review*, also noting "the surprisingly large audience." *The Diapason*, said the event "will long be remembered," and gave a "Bravo to Christopher Houlihan for taking on such a massive project, and for carrying it off with so much intelligence, artistry, and communicative power."

Looking back over the long history of PTCA during my era, it is a satisfaction not only to have helped launch the performance careers of some really fine organists, but also to have played a role in restoring Louis Vierne and his companion organ symphonists to a status of renewed prominence in this country, as they so unquestionably deserved.

Christopher Houlihan (center) in 2011 outside Notre Dame de Paris where he had just had the thrill of performing on Vierne's Cavaillé-Coll organ, backed by some of his fans who made the trip to France for the occasion. The white caps were emblazoned "Houli Fan." His agent, Phillip Truckenbrod, is standing far right.

9 Eye of the Beholder

Life has a disconcerting way of taking complete strangers and casting them together as co-stars in some little drama or another. Karen McFarlane and I by personality, temperament, geography, and interests were unlikely prospects for even meeting each other. And if we had met under other circumstances it's a decent bet neither of us would have noticed or remembered.

Yet now, both of us retired and living several states apart, we have each other as indelible sub-plots in our career stories. Nothing either of us ever did had a determinative effect on the other, and yet for years on end almost anything either of us did somehow was reflected in and colored the other's world. This left us related somehow, but the nature and structure of the relationship defied any quick name. Were we still strangers?: no, but yes at the same time. Were we colleagues?: yes, and no. Were we friends?: yes, and no; at least friendly acquaintances. Were we enemies?: no, but we may have circled around each other apprehensively, wary of any signs of trouble. We each had turf to defend, and the other seemed like a prime candidate to attempt an invasion of some not quite defined sort. A vague threat even if no threatening moves were made.

She and I were not the only agents who specialized in organist performers during our mutual heyday, and yet the others seemed to operate in an obscure haze. At least I didn't pay much attention to them, and I can't imagine that Karen did either. Why, then, did we pay attention to each other? Probably because we both identified with our roles with full professional commitment. Probably because we were both ambitious. Maybe because we were both *prima donnas* who would have really preferred to have the stage to ourselves. In any case, we saw each other as the "competition."

Everyone in organ circles seemed to feel that Karen and I must have been bitter rivals; maybe even mutually hated enemies. We were within a few months of each other in age, and we headed what were generally perceived to be the two top agencies for organist performers, or 'concert organists,' during our active careers. Karen had taken over, with the help of Fred Swann, the long established Lilian Murtagh agency when the older woman retired, but actually Karen had formed an earlier agency while living

Organists & Me

in Texas with her first husband. I had formed a similar agency at about the same time (actually somewhat earlier, I think) at first under a neutral name. Karen eventually changed her agency's name to her own, as eventually also did I to mine. Thus in actuality, both agencies had remarkably similar origins, histories and profiles. And thus, in the eyes of many organists, she and I must have been the greatest of rivals.

The odd thing of it was that in many ways we were closer than anyone was prepared to believe because we both had almost identical professional experiences and duties, and we were thus the only ones who really knew what it was like to be in the other's shoes. Whether we would have found each other interesting as friends in another setting is difficult to guess because we related only professionally. We did, however, share many cordial moments both before, and then after, she became the first to retire. And I have a nice note in my files that she sent to me once from her hospital room outlining her prognosis after a frightening illness. So whatever term would best express our relationship, "enemies" is not it.

Our styles and personalities were markedly different, however, which I'm sure fed the flames of certitude that we must hate each other with a passion. And admittedly there was an incident or two along the way which indeed stretched the bounds of civility a tad.

St. Paul's Cathedral choir just before setting off on American tour.

During one of the AGO national conventions I confronted her for what had been reported to me as her badmouthing the Choir of St. Paul's Cathedral, London, (men and boys) which at the time I represented and was touring in this country.

She was said to have been uninhibitedly spreading her opinion that this choir was not worthy of the same attention which should be given to other English choirs which she just happened to represent at the time. I suggested that it could be a good idea if I talked only about the performers I represented and that she talked only about her performers. She assured me that it was her "obligation" to let potential presenters know that the St. Paul's Choir was not up to snuff (only in more colorful language).

48

Eye of the Beholder

Then, years later, she was arranging tours in the U.S. herself for that same St. Paul's Choir even though it had the same director and many of the same adult members. So evidentially it could be concluded that the agent who represented the choir made as much of a difference in its artistic worthiness as did the person who directed it and trained its trebles. This convention conversation was managed without any raised voices, but also without any change of opinion by either her or me. So, maybe the name of the relationship could fairly be termed "business rivals," but "enemies" would still have been a vast over-statement. The context in which we were operating was simply too small and cozy to allow us to indulge in hatred; it was more like 'friends with certain misgivings'.

> BUCKINGHAM PALACE
>
> The Very Reverend Eric Evans,
> The Dean of St. Paul's.
>
> I send my sincere thanks to you, the Chapter, Organists, Vicars Choral and Choristers of St. Paul's Cathedral for your kind message of loyal greetings, sent on the occasion of your tour of the United States of America.
>
> As Patron of the Choir School Foundation I was delighted to receive this message and to read about the tour. I send my best wishes to you all for a very enjoyable and successful occasion.
>
> ELIZABETH R.
>
> 15th April, 1993.

So Karen and I had our tensions but ultimately it was just the reality of business which made us commercial rivals. I have no doubt that many times along the way either of us would have been elated to learn the other planned to retire, but at no time along the way would either of us have been even slightly happy to learn the other was dead or seriously ill. In fact, during one period when Karen was hospitalized for a time, I sent her a plant for her room. This seemed an odd move to many in the AGO, and several of the members of her roster of artists thanked me as though considering for the first time the possibility that perhaps I was not the devil incarnate.

In the long run Karen and I probably ignored each other more than we were even aware of each other on a routine basis, as we went about our individual work which demanded complete concentration. For the most part what I was aware of Karen doing came just from reading the AGO journal. The great rivalry was mostly a product of a collective AGO imagination which needed its soap operas as does any group. The rivalry flourished mostly in the eyes of others.

While during most of my agency time I felt we and the McFarlane group were pretty much on an equal footing, it must be admitted that things didn't start that way and it took some work and time for us to climb up to their level. The advantage of her agency during the early years was not something she had plotted or even earned by an individual effort, but the result of inheritance. It came about by circumstance, as does so much of anyone's life and career.

The whole idea of an agency in this country devoted especially to concert organists originated with a French-Canadian, Bernard LaBerge, who later became a naturalized U.S. citizen. He used his connections to bring over the leading French organist performers of the late 19th and early 20th centuries, and their titles, exalted in American eyes (*Notre Dame de Paris*, etc.), made them successful touring musicians in that period when the organ was still a highly popular classical music instrument here. LaBerge also added to his roster some American names, one being Claire Coci whom he married, and another being Virgil Fox who was part of that wedding party. Then after LaBerge the business was (eventually, after a period as the New York agency Colbert-LaBerge) taken over by his secretary, Lilian Murtagh, who added some Americans to the roster and carried it on under her own name from 1962 to 1976.

By then Fred Swann had taken over the Riverside Church post from Virgil Fox and was a member of the Murtagh roster. When Lilian became ill and prepared to retire, as I understood it, Fred arranged for Karen McFarlane, then his music secretary at the Riverside Church, to make a number of trips up to Canaan, Connecticut, to help the older woman close shop and to learn the business. So it was that Karen took a big step up in the agency business, from her own small agency to a ready-made roster of artists who were already highly regarded in this country, and with an agency bearing a by then legendary name.

Did that give her an advantage? Yes, decidedly so, and there's no point not to admit it. I was a guy with a strange sounding family name whom few in the field had ever heard of and my initial artists were young and little known on the wider scene. So Karen overnight had the upper hand in a big way and, I don't think it's unfair to say, for a long time appeared to regard herself to be the more important and credible agent as a result.

But, unlike a number of other small attempts at building an agency in the organ field along the way, our agency didn't go away after taking on the uphill slog. We were not the 'establishment' at that point but among the younger performers who clamored for a place at the table were many very fine organists who gradually helped me build a roster of genuine weight and potential. Karen, to my observation in those early days, may have been somewhat paralyzed by holding the winning hand; it robbed her of flexibility and forced her to think in "establishment" rather than "innovative" terms.

She had a pre-existing name and a legacy to uphold, and I had only the obligation to build and grow. So PTCA steadily climbed up to the same

Eye of the Beholder

lofty perch by dint of hard and persistent work, by a willingness to frequently take a chance, and to give many younger performers the chances they needed. This juxtaposition created a rather odd long-range drift by the two agencies with regard to adding new artists. She began with widely

THE STAR-LEDGER, Tuesday, June 8, 1971

Music in Jersey

A friend remembers Marcel Dupre

By PHILLIP TRUCKENBROD

The death of Marcel Dupre last week in Paris has been felt with special pain by a Jersey woman who was a long time friend and student of the famed organist and the wife of his concert manager in this country.

Dupre was regarded throughout the world as the greatest organ virtuoso of this century. He was especially noted for his improvisations and was a prolific composer as well.

Dr. Claire Coci, herself a concert organist who operates the American Academy of Music in Tenafly and teaches music at New York's Union Theological Seminary, first met Dupre when she became engaged to his countryman Bernard LaBerge.

LaBerge later emigrated to the U.S. and founded a concert management agency specializing in organists in a day when the organ was very popular with the concert going public here.

* * *

LaBerge brought Dupre to New York for his American debut in 1921 and the Frenchman's popularity as a performer became legendary overnight.

On that first tour Dupre performed 94 concerts in 85 American cities, and according to LaBerge's widow, "never performed to less than a standing-room-only audience and never received less than a standing ovation" during any of his tours in this country.

Dr. Coci, who always refers to her late husband by his last name, said, "LaBerge could never bring him over here often enough to satisfy the demand."

Last month Dupre celebrated his 85th birthday and special rounds of concerts and receptions were planned in London and Paris to commemorate the event.

Dr. Coci flew to Paris for her friend's birthday and recalls with affection sitting on the organ bench with him as he played the regular Sunday morning Masses at the Church of Saint-Sulpice in Paris where he had been organist for over 65 years.

Because of Dupre's fame around the world, the church has become something of a shrine for organ music fans and in recent years Sunday morning Masses began with a welcoming sentence spoken by a priest which acknowledged that most of those in the pews had come to hear the organist.

"On behalf of Marcel Dupre, welcome to Saint-Sulpice," the priest began.

It was a nostalgic trip for Dr. Coci, who spent most of her stay at the Dupre's home in Meudon, a suburb of the French capital.

* * *

She recalled earlier summers spent with her husband at that home as guests of Dupre. "He and LaBerge were like brothers," she said. "They were closer than one would ever suspect a manager and artist to be."

It was in the Meudon home, complete with its own recital hall seating over 200 and a large four manual pipe organ, that many festivities marking Dupre's birthday were held.

"For several years on Dupre's birthday I have wanted to go to Paris to be with him again," said the Jersey musician. "This year I had an intuition that I should sacrifice the time and money and actually do it."

Only a few days after returning to Tenafly, Dr. Coci and fans of organ music throughout the world were stunned to learn of Dupre's death.

"I waited until after the funeral and then phoned his widow," said Dr. Coci. "She told me he had played the Mass at Saint-Sulpice a week ago Sunday as he had done all those years whether ill or healthy, and come home to take his usual Sunday afternoon nap.

"He died as she was sitting next to the bed talking with him," she said. "The improvisation that morning had been 'wonderful' his wife told me."

Dr. Coci will share her memories of the legendary Dupre on Thursday evening over WSOU, Seton Hall University FM radio at 89.5, on the "O r g a n Masterworks" program beginning at 9:05 p.m.

She will also perform a memorial concert for her former teacher on June 24 at Trinity Church, Broadway and Wall Street in New York, at 12:45 p.m.

* * *

Among the items she will discuss during the Thursday evening radio program will be Dupre's home pipe organ.

"It was especially built for his improvisations," she said, "and the standard keyboard was not enough, so four extra notes were added to each of the four keyboards making them probably the only 65 note organ manuals in the world."

Dupre was a "very warm, very docile, very human and loving man," according to Dr. Coci.

Video Viewpoint

Stations playing it safe

By CECIL SMITH

HOLLYWOOD — The feeling here was that the Federal Communications Commission ruling to cut 12 hours a week off network prime time to try to stimulate local and independent production was like declaring open season for TV gamesmanship.

Game shows are cheap to make and relatively easy to do, in comparison with dramas or comedies or even variety hours. A bonanza of gamesmanship was expected to flood the air.

It hasn't, and I went up to see a master of the trade, Chuck Barris, to ask why. Barris, a smallish but ruggedly built man, who moves with the catlike grace of an athlete, a good flyweight, said the FCC chickened out on its own ruling and killed the market.

"When they agreed to give local station's a year's grace in which they could do old network programs or reruns in this new prime time, they violated every reason to have the rule," he said. "Stations across the country are buying up Lawrence Welk and Hee Haw and Lassie in syndication or reruns of all those shows the networks dropped. They can go with proved products; why take a chance with new shows?"

* * *

Chuck, whose "Dating Game" and "Newlywed Game" lost their prime time slots in the ABC reshuffle but are still daytime shows on the network, said his company made three pilots for new game shows, "Cop Out, "Dream Girl" and "Parent Game," but decided to shelve them.

"Six or eight months from now," he said, "we'll know which way to go. Either the FCC will back down and apologize and give the prime time back to the networks, or they will get tough and demand local stations fill that time the following season with a new product. Then we'll have to get out and sell."

The prospect is not unappealing to Chuck. "It will be like 1951-52 selling again, where a guy put his show under his arm and went on the road and sold it, station by station. Something went out of television when you had to have a network for a partner."

* * *

Chuck is from the network scene. He was director of daytime programs for ABC when he submitted his first game show, "People Pickers," "a known artists and thus, almost by necessity, took a highly exclusive stance about adding new talent. Then gradually with time, at least to my perception, started to become more liberal in adding roster members. At least so by the time John McElliott took over. I, on the other hand, and also by necessity, began by accepting most candidates who demonstrated genuine performance talent and determination (plus interest in our work). Then over time as my agency grew in recognition and stature, I gradually adopted a much more exclusive approach, almost by necessity. In that odd way, it seemed, the two agencies were both paralleling each other and at the same time experiencing a cross-over of business philosophy.

Part of our (perhaps necessary) openness to new talent and new approaches included attempting to keep a blind eye when it came to race. The business of organ performance and representation in this country had been a white person's game as far back as anyone could recall, with a few black organists along the way pretty much consigned to the sidelines. Torrence, to give him the credit he deserves, had been willing, early-on in my time to give Herndon Spillman a place on his roster. Herndon soon went off to Europe for an extended stay to study with Maurice Duruflé, and by the time he returned home Torrence had closed his agency and entered his Russian exile. Herndon turned to us, and I, as a pious and practicing Democrat and, hopefully, a decent person, take some pride in having agreed to represent the first African-American organist on the roster of a major American agency.

Then happenstance added another fine African-American organist of performance caliber to our roster. The AGO, RCO, and RCCO (see the definition of abbreviations at the back of the book) at the time jointly sponsored something they called the International Congress of Organists (ICO) which was held several times in England and twice in North America, in Philadelphia and in Montreal, before disappearing. The Philadelphia organizers asked us to be involved, and I suggested that we could augment the prizes for the planned performance and improvisation competitions by giving the winners a place on our roster. A young man from New York City won both of the competitions, and thus we got to add David Hurd to our offerings, and to acquire a good friend in the bargain.

Later as we grew beyond just organists, we added the New England Spiritual Ensemble (later "The National Spiritual Ensemble") which became one of our most successful choral groups. We evidently tapped into a yearning among some of the AGO types who had felt short-changed previously. One of them phoned me to extoll how great all of this was, and how "as far as I'm concerned the other agency should just close shop in disgrace."

Eye of the Beholder

The 'rivalry' thing kept turning up in odd ways. Malcolm Williamson was friendly with a young woman organist of some name-recognition in the field, and he determined he was going to steer her to the PTCA roster. In the end she decided to opt for Karen's agency, and she had the personal backing of a man with enough heft in the field to make that happen fairly automatically. I had not been totally sure she was a good fit for us in any case, but the pressure from Malcolm had been enough to prompt her to send me a note apologizing for going in the other direction, because "I so admire Karen as a church music secretary." I never quite got the connection.

It would be interesting (for me, at least) to know how Karen, and then her successor, John McElliott, viewed this process of many years. I do think they changed their perspectives to some degree, because their roster gradually became less dependent on the old established artist names which had originally given it top billing—of course, regardless of their attitudes, nature had a gradual hand in clearing the decks as well. It was my observation that after John took over, that agency began to be far more open to new talent, as I mentioned above, to the point that during my last years in the business I thought he might be going too far and adding names too rapidly. But I also took that as another sign that the field of organ performance was becoming increasingly challenging, as indeed I could hardly fail to see for myself.

I've not specifically asked either of them for their perspectives (they may want to write their own books in due course; I did, however, offer both the chance to contribute something to this book if they would like, but they declined) but something Karen said to me some years ago at an AGO convention had signaled to me that she had finally accepted me as a peer: "You've paid your dues."

Others in the organ scene most likely continued to see and enjoy the spectacle of the 'great rivalry.' One of the most bizarre outcroppings of this was a visit to my office by Karen's first husband, the "McFarlane" of her name, who sought representation on our roster. I think maybe he wanted to perform with his current wife as a vocal duo, but not as an organist in any case. Anyway, like an astute politician, he tried to sell me on the idea that this would be an explosive turning-of-the-tables, and would somehow catapult PTCA over any remaining advantage held by Karen's agency. Being human, I did find the idea sort of amusing for a few hours, but then decided we were already past the point of needing to correct any remaining imagined disadvantage. Besides, I had always rather liked Karen despite our enforced competitiveness, and just did not see that starting a range war would accomplish anything productive or healthy.

Organists & Me

So a lid was kept on "the great rivalry" most of the time, and the flames never got too much out of control. That does not mean that there weren't moments of flare up however. The Parisian organist and composer Jean Guillou sent an emissary to my office asking that he be admitted to our agency roster for work in the U.S. We had not solicited his interest in any way. Karen, on reliable authority, was reported to have reacted with shock. "I would have taken him on, why didn't he contact me?" In other words, Guillou had already exhibited a misunderstanding of how things were supposed to work over here.

Thereafter the New York City AGO chapter named Guillou its annual "Performer of the Year" and his award recital was scheduled. Following it at the reception, I have it from an impeccably reliable witness in the room at the time that a prominent member of the McFarlane roster pulled Guillou aside and told him, "You can do better than that agency," that is, better than PTCA. The rest of the conversation was not reported to me, but it's not too difficult to fill in the blanks, or the motive.

So circumstances and business ambitions kept Karen and me on each other's radar, and quite naturally at that, because during those years we were really the only peer group either of us had inside the AGO. But true as that was, the mutual interest fell short of an obsession on either side. I found little bits of hear-say interesting along the way, but arms-length sort of interesting. Mostly I was eager to understand how someone else might conceive of and go about promotion and *esprit de corps* building in almost the identical context in which I was operating. I remember that at one of Karen's significant birthdays her then husband, the organ builder Chick Holtkamp, threw a big party for her which was labeled "Backstage Madam." All the roster members, I was told by one of them, were asked to chip in to commission new compositions for the event. That sounded intriguing and innovative, but I was so far removed from her orbit that it's not easy to assess the impact. I guess, in a way, that sums up our relationship: keeping an eye on each other but never being close enough to really fully appreciate the other, and always too busy to put much effort into trying in any case.

Why the 'great rivalry,' perceived or real, was of any interest to anyone other than Karen and me I never had a real grasp of. But it did seem to be a sideshow that fascinated some AGO types. As an example, we represented John Walker, then organist of the Riverside Church in New York, a position made famous because it had been held for many years by Virgil Fox. John Walker was Fox's second successor in the position and had inherited an assistant organist who was represented by McFarlane. One day an out-of-the-blue caller congratulated me on representing the head organist of the church while Karen represented only the assistant organist, and told me how amusing he found that situation. I thought that this was a lot of analysis to go through to assign a leading agency status in one's imagination, especially when organists kept moving around and changing church positions in any case. But it was clear that Karen and I had an audience whom we were keeping amused just by our routine business dealings, and that the audience evidently picked and rooted for favorites as if it were a horse race with betting options.

10 Organizational Identity Confusion

The 'rivalry' legend did, however, in my perception say something about the collective mentality of the AGO. The organization always seemed to me to be trying to figure itself out, and its members seemed never to be completely sure of who they were professionally or exactly why the organization was needed, or what it was supposed to stand for. Originally education was one of its key functions, and while it still was granting its own degrees and certificates, the opportunities to study organ in regular schools had proliferated to the point that the AGO degrees were now just frosting on the cake. Some treated it as merely an organization of professionals in the same field, almost as just a social club. Some wanted it to be a union, but I think most seemed to think of it as a quasi-religious organization; an extension of organized Christianity (although there was always a small number of Jewish musicians in its membership).

Partially this confusion probably stemmed from the fact that the AGO was forced to serve a great variety of people who were connected with the organ in widely divergent ways. Most were church musicians on one level or another, but some were professors and academics with or without a church position on the side (usually with), some were organ builders and technicians, some were simply enthusiasts who loved the instrument and its music whether or not they could play a note themselves. Some were involved with the organ as a performance instrument rather than as a church instrument, including both professional performers and agents for professional performers. The AGO was forced, by virtue of the relatively small numbers involved, to serve as a catch-all organization giving succor to a very wide variety of involvements and motivations. Since most of those involved had occupational (professional) ties to churches, and did things like playing organ preludes and directing choirs for a living, when they came together I guess it just seemed natural to keep doing those things and to continue to place them in the context of a church-like service.

This "catholic" aspect may have ultimately been a strength, but often it manifested itself as weakness. We argued about what kind of instruments organs were supposed to be, with sometimes extremely strong opinions endorsing tracker, or electro-pneumatic, or electronic machines and usually to the exclusion of each other. We argued in the same way about the

Organizational Identity Confusion

superiority of very early musical literature, or romantic era literature, or modern literature of the organ, which in turn left us to argue about who the best performers were, frequently based on what era of literature or type of instrument they favored. We argued about whether transcriptions were acceptable as organ literature. Some usually unvoiced but nonetheless palpable tension also revolved around whether the organization belonged to the church organists, or whether the others (enthusiasts, builders, etc.) had a legitimate stake as well.

The 'religiosity' tension tended to impose 'niceness' as an AGO standard, which was pleasant for us as people, but perhaps not a great contributor to the cause of professionalism. In my view this attitude of not wanting to hurt anyone's feelings sometimes opened the back door to mediocrity (unintentionally and indirectly). I've observed this factor at work in the way performers were selected for conventions, competitions were judged, committee assignments were made, and a lot of varied decisions were made. AGO 'niceness,' as I observed it, seemed at times to be a barrier to the rise of the best talent and capacity among us, and mostly just a mechanism for preventing some of the weakest and least talented from feeling too unhappy or neglected. The AGO was treated by most members as an organization of equals, but of course its members were not at all equal in their various levels of talent or commitment to the cause.

To me the most interesting, although often pointless, tension was the uncertainty as to whether the AGO was primarily a sort of union for church musicians or was itself a quasi-religious organization. This was not helped by the fact that it had a decidedly religious motto ("*Soli Deo Gloria*") which whether Bach's or not could be rationally viewed as out of place for an organization of such mixed intention and purpose.

Another hint in the same direction was that the organization had, and still has, a chaplain. This person, appointed by the national president, used to have a regular column in every issue of TAO, although this may not be the case anymore (the pattern seems to vary quite a bit now). Other groups of musicians got along just fine without chaplains. Why did the AGO need one? Usually this person was not an organist himself and thus could not make a musical contribution. The only explanation I could ever come up with was that the AGO saw and defined itself in ecclesiastical terms—that was without any doubt its comfort zone.

AGO national conventions opened with an event which, if not intended as an actual religious service, was so cleverly disguised as one that the distinction hardly mattered. These ceremonies started with a procession of vested officials and dignitaries during an organ prelude, then proceeded on with invocations (prayers), hymns, and choir anthems. Any distinction between these convocations and a religious service was lost on me, although I doubt anyone else saw any incongruity at all.

One national convention (probably more than one; they tend to run together in my memory) also featured daily chapel services (overt and unapologetic religious services) during the week led by ordained clergy from various denominations. As you may have gathered, by then I was a very long way from my own clergy days and never attended these religious services. Still, their presence colored the complexion of the convention.

So I sailed along attending one after another of these AGO conventions, never appreciating why the religious aspects were needed or what they contributed. They made me a little uncomfortable, however. The average AGO member, on the other hand, probably could not conceive of an organizational convention as anything but a quasi-religious event. The comfort-zone and self-identity of the AGO was definitely vested in religion, so I was probably the odd-man out.

Then, on top of that, there were the wildly divergent attitudes as to whether church musicians were simply professional employees of ecclesiastical organizations, or themselves quasi-clergy who must maintain and espouse strictly 'orthodox' theological opinions. As a former clergyman it may have been a lot easier for me to draw a distinction between these poles, but for musicians actively involved in "the ministry" of music it seemed to pose an identity challenge.

In most denominations being employed by a church to offer specific services did not mandate that the employee had to hold, and uphold, specific theological tenets—not for the church janitor, and not for the church organist either. Often enough a church musician grew up in a particular tradition/denomination, and then was employed by a parish of a different ecclesiastical tradition. But there were always a lot of these organists who, as part of the "ministry team" of their parish, felt that they needed to be junior theologians who defended one approach over others whether they had much of a grasp of the theology involved or not. To me that seemed like they were carrying an unnecessary burden, or on the other end of the scale, claiming an unearned status. It seemed so much easier to just say the pastor has his job (or today probably "her" job), and I have mine.

My position was on the sidelines of most of this and I was an observer with some vested business interest but not much other skin in the game. And I sat pretty much on the sidelines trying to uphold and encourage what I felt would be a more professional orientation for the organization and its conventions, but with no official capacity; just a bit of influence here and there but nothing with enough organizational clout to actually make a difference. There were, however, times when I got dragged into the caldron of organizational uncertainty and unshakable contrasting opinions, religious or not.

THE AGENT AS DISCIPLINARIAN AND DISCIPLINED

My job was to represent performers (concert artists, whether also church musicians or not) and to try to make them visible and attractive to the (mostly) church musicians who might book them to perform on (mostly) church concert series or special occasions. The extent to which I was doing an adequate job was a subject many AGO members were not shy about informing me.

Searching for something a touch unusual to avoid the sterility of stereotypical player-at-instrument photos, I once decided to use a photo of a pianist we represented, Paul Bisaccia, lying on top of his grand piano in formal attire but with one knee bent so that his shoe touched the piano lid-- heresy, evidently, in the eyes of some musicians. I was immediately subjected to emails lamenting how greatly I disrespected the sacred instrument (or was it the piece of furniture?). Anyway, the musicians were determined to keep me in line and were not shy about telling me when I went wrong.

There was also afoot the strange notion that the most effective way to control the performers themselves was issuing threats via their agent, or threatening the agent himself—either way the agent seemed to be seen as an effective tool to correct, control, or to exact revenge.

One of my most venerable and distinguished roster organists had, admittedly, a fondness for the bottle which made him a "colorful" participant in AGO conventions. At one evening afterglow at one of the seemingly endless parade of conventions which I can barely tell apart in memory, he was speaking without inhibition and apparently insulted a female AGO regular. Her friends immediately launched an email campaign trying to persuade me that I should drop the performer from my roster of artists.

The interesting aspect of this to me was that these good AGO folks evidently felt the loss of agency representation would be an appropriate punishment for the man in question, and that it was the duty of the agent to administer this punishment. There had always been an underground theme in AGO circles that being represented by one of the large agencies was in and of itself a credential with value, and that it could thus be used as a cudgel for enforcement of expected norms, whether those norms belonged to the agent and artist or not.

Some of the 'enforcers' who frequented my inbox sometimes did not bother directing me to threaten an artist with loss of representation, but would instead threaten the agency directly with loss of business. "I'll (We'll) never use your agency again," was a frequent declaration. The quasi-humorous irony was that this threat never came from anyone who actually had booked my artists, but invariably from a person whom I had never

Organists & Me

heard of and who most definitely had never been a customer in the first place. Sometimes the threat was made on behalf of an entire AGO chapter, but when so, always a tiny chapter which most likely would never be able to seriously consider booking a professional performer regardless of circumstances.

Likely the most interesting (perhaps confounding) incidence along these lines occurred when a member of our roster, Christopher Houlihan, decided he wanted to experiment with breaking the mold for photos of musical artists, which could admittedly get pretty stereotypical and dull. He tapped into a trend then (and still) current in musical and artistic circles of photos with the performer barefoot. I have no real idea what this was supposed to accomplish, but examples were everywhere one could look at the time—in magazines, on TV, in advertisements. He didn't ask me before investing in these photos and I didn't react when I first saw them. I just thought, well this is a little adventuresome given the staid context of the AGO but let's go ahead and try to shake things up a bit.

The photos, casual but in good taste I thought, were few and used only sparingly and for a limited time while I was still with the agency. But shake things up I guess they did. I was immediately hit with an agitated email, forwarded by *The American Organist* editor which had been sent to him by an angry AGO member who demanded that such pornography should be rejected by TAO (it was paid advertising, not editorial content, by the way).

The letter to the editor (not for publication, and without a copy to me) said, in effect, that the writer was utterly scandalized that a church publication (*ahem!*) would publish such trash and that TAO should no longer accept our agency advertising (we were the publication's largest advertiser and had been for many years, and the executive director himself told me this was very important income for the organization). The email to the editor also indicated neither the writer nor the writer's AGO chapter would ever do business with my agency again.

Of course, neither he nor his chapter (very small and rural) ever had booked one of our artists in the first place and the likelihood that they would have in the future, regardless of his threat, must have approached statistical zero. So I was spared shaking in my boots, but I also thought I could use this as a teaching and clarifying opportunity by replying directly to the writer and to the score of people he had copied.

Organizational Identity Confusion

I tried to explain that the photos had nothing whatsoever to do with church. They were part of advertising belonging to TAO's dual role as a professional journal for the pipe organ as sheerly a musical instrument, not as a church instrument. We were not offering the performer involved as an organist for church services, but as a concert performer. I doubt the AGO guy was convinced, but he did not reply to me in any case. By the way, I then made it successfully all the way to retirement without any bookings from his AGO chapter, and the artist involved rose to become one of the acknowledged performance giants of the field.

What impressed me about this episode is how it put into relief the confusion which the AGO and its journal had about the role they should be performing. It also highlighted the narrow rigidity in which so many church organists tried to decipher their roles.

Bare feet in church was hardly the stuff of scandal, even though we had not been advocating that in any way in the first place, and none of the photos were taken in a church.

All over the world, and from the earliest days of church structures, in Roman Catholic and Orthodox as well as Protestant settings, there have been naked feet both depicted and in fact. I have observed literally countless naked toes on statues and in paintings in churches, plus several uncovered female breasts and even an occasional undraped penis to boot. Traditional churches have a foot washing ceremony on Thursday of Holy Week which requires—gasp!—some people to remove their shoes and socks, and to do so inside a church. I almost hope the chapter dean from rural wherever who wrote in to threaten our agency doesn't venture too far afield geographically in life for fear he might lose his sense of righteous indignation by walking into some church which doesn't hue to his particular standards of righteousness.

The incident simply reminded me again that, so far as I could see, the AGO had difficulty seeing itself as anything other than some sort of version of church, and a fairly narrow version at that. The way we tried to accommodate diversity was to keep tightening the restrictions so that we were only aware of and admitted to only the most basic parts that we agreed on rather than delighting in any newer variations on the theme. AGO, it appeared, was supposed to be an ideologically safe harbor rather than a challenge to growth.

From my experience one did not have to scratch the AGO too deeply to come up with members who believed that taking away artistic representation was appropriate punishment for imagined (or sometimes actual) infractions, or that damaging the business of an agency was an appropriate response for the perceived failings of one of its roster members. The good old religious virtue of revenge for daring not to be as upright as one considered oneself was apparently as alive and well as ever and had found a home in our circles (I guess we were human after all).

Probably I've left no ambiguity about my perspective on the AGO as a religious organization, but just in case: I don't think it is, I don't think it needs to be, nor do I think it should try to be. I don't even quite understand what the religious aspect contributes to the organization. Most organists needed to have at least some income from church work to survive financially in those days, but that did not, and still does not, mean the organ can't or shouldn't stand on its own as a musical instrument. And it used to puzzle me a bit that these good people who spent so much time participating in church services should then want to use what was essentially vacation time to participate in yet more church-like services at AGO conventions.

(Of course I do understand and appreciate the value of members of a given professional group comparing notes and seeing how their peers handle various circumstances. But if that aspect is emphasized maybe a name change for the sake of honesty is called for: The American Guild of Church Organists, or maybe even The American Guild of Church Choir Directors, which publishes a journal named *The American Church Organist*.)

By the way, I need to make it clear that these comments about the AGO's role are merely my observations. They do not necessarily represent the opinion of my successor or any of the artists I have represented along the way. I may have been one of the very few, or even possibly the only one, to be at all disturbed by the blending together of professional, organizational and religious concerns. Everyone else seemed to be either happy or unconcerned with the ways of the AGO.

And it's possible, too, that you may think I'm the one who was confused rather than the organization. I had worked as an ordained clergyman before becoming an artist's agent, after all. Presumably I was squarely in the corner of organized religion, and should have cheered any group which upheld and encouraged organized religion. I don't have a ready, short, and snappy retort to that, and I doubt this is the place for an extended effort at self-analysis. So let's compromise by just saying that I might have been yet another of the complicated characters who populated the organ field and peppered it with bits of (hopefully ultimately charming) eccentricity.

11 Business Perspectives

While I could easily see the AGO identity struggle which pitted the religious and the secular against each other in what seemed a never ending tug of war, it was harder to see the 'log in my own eye.' I was, after all, a guy who had been drawn to religion professionally before making my home among the organists. My instincts were to try to see the best in people and to believe what they said about themselves. I tended to take people at face value reflexively. That was a helpful mental position for a clergyman, but a fairly unhelpful position for a businessman.

Also, I had an odd handicap. I was an Iowan and deeply afflicted with the legendary "Iowa-nice" way of seeing life: never risk offending anyone by disagreeing with them because that might make the other guy unhappy. Minnesotans like to brag that they have the same disease. Maybe so. It may be a characteristic of the Midwest in general. This perspective, like religion itself, put a premium on looking out for the underdog and trying to take everybody at face value. It also meant that one would not contradict another person, or openly challenge his evaluation of himself, except in the most extreme of circumstances.

In any case, it took me some time to realize I wasn't a pastor anymore; that I now had a business to operate and that there were people who depended on it. I very gradually realized that many of my instincts were naïve in this new setting. I wasn't in business to nurture weak personalities who wanted to be concert organists despite insufficient real talent or lack of stage presence. I was in business to lend a hand to those who were the real talents in the field—to those who actually had a chance to become the leading performers of the day.

And it took some time to realize that feeling an obligation to help the weakest among us was not doing them any favors either, because it merely encouraged them in an unrealistic pursuit of glory they would never actually attain. Furthermore, tending to the weakest cheated those who really deserved my full attention, and it cheated me and the agency as well. Then there was my obligation to the presenters who were our customers. To give weak performers a billing that appeared to put them on an equal level with the potential stars was offering a confused picture to those presenters who wanted to give their audiences the best the field had to offer.

Organists & Me

In short, I wasn't in the God-business anymore (nor for that matter an Iowan anymore either), and it was not the agency's business to cradle people who would like to be concert caliber artists, but did not have the raw materials to match their hopes. This is not an especially easy transition to make for a church person.

Much of this was brought home to me in two somewhat dramatic interactions with guys who asked to be represented by the agency. At the Chartres organ performance competitions I attended for many seasons in France there was always a tall German man of striking appearance who frequently chose to sit next to me at the awards dinners. He was not an organist himself but was there because he had arranged for a group of local Lions Clubs in Germany to sponsor a prize for the competition, given each season to the competitor the judges felt gave the best Bach performance. He was a fine musician, however—a pianist with several commercial recordings (I had examples of them in hand) and a healthy performance career going in Europe (at least so he claimed).

He was also, he told me, a Grammy Award recipient. I was duly impressed and gave him the agency berth he asked for. I arranged a first American tour for him of several highly visible and well paid performances. He arrived on schedule, looked at the piano at the first venue, found it not up to his standards, melted down, and flew immediately back to Germany. This left me with a super-sized mess on my hands, but we were able to substitute one or another of our other roster pianists for most of the venues. Okay, one big lesson learned, although not yet the one which I could have side-stepped had I not been so trusting.

One of the other pianists on our roster, although happy to accept some of the work from the scuttled tour, was also growing increasingly jealous. He was annoyed about someone on the roster having a Grammy when he knew, of course, that it really should have been him. John and I were in Paris for John's second performance at Notre Dame de Paris (many years before the infamous fire, of course) when the other pianist telephoned me in the middle of the night to inform me that he was sure the German did not actually have a Grammy at all.

When I got home I set about finding out for myself, and the jealous pianist turned out to be correct. I then confronted the German, and he said in self-defense that he had long assumed he had won the Grammy because friends in America had congratulated him on the achievement. The most credit I could give him was the slight possibility that he might have been nominated for a Grammy and had naively assumed that equaled being awarded one (or at least that his friends *thought* he had been nominated; the Grammy office said no, not even a nomination was involved). I had been naïve to accept his claim on face value, and if he were being honest he was naïve to believe he had been awarded a Grammy without having it physically in hand—a sort of double-layer naivety which I might have avoided if I'd been a little more secular in my approach.

Unfortunately this was not the last time I had to learn a similar lesson. One among the endless stream of organists who applied for representation by the agency was an Italian who claimed that he was the organist of St. Peter's with the clear intention of having that read as St. Peter's Basilica in the Vatican. The applicant also asked me to keep his title under my hat for a few more weeks because it had not yet been announced and the former organist still did not realize he was on the way out. Here's a case where I got tripped up because I knew just enough to imagine how this could be the case, and therefore was blinded to what should have been a healthy skepticism. In other words, I knew just enough to remain ignorant.

I knew, for example, that the person who was indeed the current organist of St. Peter's was not seen by many of his peers as an especially outstanding organ talent, and that he rarely performed outside the Vatican; he was mostly just a good service player and choir accompanist, which was all the St. Peter's position really needed. I also knew that the newly installed Pope was himself a pianist and something of a German perfectionist. So, two and two together equaled that the Pope had taken a hand in trying to improve the Vatican's musical standards and had appointed a bigger talent as organist of St. Peter's. The story I conjured in my head from the proffered pieces which seemed to make so much sense was not only intriguing, but seemed to offer a performer with great potential in the market-place, a modern day Fernando Germani hopefully.

Yet I was level-headed enough to require meeting and talking with this organist in person before going ahead with any professional relationship. And at this point I was hindered because there just wasn't enough money available for me to go to Rome to see for myself. But I was already scheduled to be in Paris in a few weeks, however, so I asked the "Vatican organist" to meet me there. We spent a long day having a meal together and by the time he returned to Rome I was convinced of his story.

Back home, however, an acquaintance told me I was wrong and that there had been no change in the Vatican organ post. He was a friend of the actual organist of St. Peter's who had repeatedly tried to convince me to represent this organist, although I'd always demurred because of the weak reputation the organist had among his peers. So I started to investigate, even to the point of calling the Apostolic Delegate (as he was then called) at the Vatican embassy in Washington DC. Sure enough, my roster applicant was an imposter.

But he was a really slick and convincing imposter. I never figured out exactly what he thought he would gain from all of this. His name would need to be announced fairly soon as the newly appointed organist of St. Peter's, which he knew was not going to happen. He could not go on very much longer before his fairy tale crashed from its own weight. And as innocent as he may have thought Americans to be, he could not have flown around this country claiming the Vatican title without the inconvenient truth emerging fairly soon; Americans were sometimes naïve, but they were hardly isolated from the rest of the world.

After I confronted the applicant with my research he put on a shocked and confused façade and continued to maintain the truth of his claim. Then the story underwent a little mutation; he was not actually the titular organist at St. Peter's but a regular staff organist, used to fill in there upon occasion. It was not even worth pursuing the truth of that claim. I was left to conclude that he must have been mentally off balance, or to use a clinical term, a nut job.

So agency work was exposing me to a lot of "interesting" characters and gradually teaching me that religious instincts of trust and compassion did not mix well with business realities. The AGO and I were struggling together to figure out the distinction between religion and the art of the organ. I don't think the AGO will ever get there. For most AGO members "church" music is their comfort zone, and for many of them being a "church organist" really means identifying as a choir director.

During my time with PTCA there was occasionally some talk among friends about trying to establish an organization and journal devoted solely to the pipe organ as a musical instrument. This would have involved organ performers interested primarily in the instrument and its literature rather than the church music aspect, organ builders, educators, and hopefully fans. Such a move would then relieve the AGO of some of the many varied roles it was forced to juggle and leave it to concentrate on church music, where its heart seemed to be already. (Some might have considered the OHS to be a step in that direction, but the emphasis there was on the instruments themselves rather than on a secular, strictly musical, employment of them.)

The problem was numbers, however, or perhaps better stated as the lack thereof. Those of us AGO members who were primarily connected for reasons other than church music were simply too few to carry a national organization of any consequence. So in the end the AGO and its journal were left to play multiple roles as they always had, serving both those primarily interested in church music *per se* as well as those who valued the organ on independent terms. The organization still seemed to me a bit deceptively named, but not intentionally deceptive. It had inherited a difficult set of roles and clients which somehow had to be integrated into a realistic whole. So, frustrating as the organization could seem at times, thank heavens we had (and still have) it.

Business Perspectives

John Rose on the Trinity College quad with the Aeolian-Skinner console from the Garden Court of the Frick Collection which traveled with him from New Jersey to Connecticut. Trinity College Chapel is in the background.

12 Personalities

Tony (Anthony Baglivi, long-time advertising manager and then editor of the AGO's journal) and Rollin Smith (a leading organist performer, as mentioned previously, but more widely known as a scholar and historian of the instrument and its literature, composers, and performers) had gradually become John and my best 'couple' friends and we spent a lot of time with them both locally and even on a long vacation driving trip to Charleston. Tony and Rollin had met at a Carnegie Hall concert some time before John and I met at a church event in the Bronx, and both couples had been together from the moment of meeting, by then for several years each.

Tony and Rollin seemed to know everyone even remotely associated with the organ in the New York area, and were the ticket to our meeting many of the luminaries and 'characters' of the scene. One Christmas period they staged a holiday party at their home in Brooklyn and invited us together with our then housemate, the prominent harpsichordist Robert Edward Smith. One of their other guests was the New York organist Calvin Hampton, known not only as a performer but as a composer. Robert, in addition to being a performer was also emerging at the time as a composer of significance.

We were standing around holding drinks in a knot of people when Tony approached and addressed a nearby guy who turned out to be Hampton. "Calvin, this is Robert Edward Smith," Tony offered, nodding to Robert and sure that the two composers would find common ground.

"How *nice* for him," Hampton managed, in the most icy and defensive condescension I've ever witnessed, before turning his back and walking away. With a personality that insecure one might have wondered how he had managed to become a significant figure on the New York church music and concert organ scene, but he did have his fans—especially a spinster woman who volunteered as his lackey. Years later, after Hampton's death, she came up to our agency booth at an AGO convention and stood flipping through the organ CDs for sale. I asked if I could help her find anything particular. "Do you have anything by Calvin Hampton?" she replied. "I only buy recordings by Calvin Hampton."

Tony and Rollin were themselves well-known and loved characters in this mix, not only for their strong professional contributions, but for their

Personalities

irrepressible personalities. Rollin, especially, was an expert at blurting out unfiltered gems which endeared him to us increasingly. At a Village restaurant one night the four of us sat eating and discussing the facts of life as we had so far discovered them. The restaurant was reputed to be 'gay' but that only meant that it was patronized also by lots of 'straights' who were sure that the gay boys could nose out the best places, and thus flocked to follow them. It was a crowded evening abuzz with lively conversation when Rollin made one of his full-voiced observations. The room seemed to fall silent for a moment, and the man in the next booth turned around to extend a "touché!" to our table.

Tony had a habit of trying to avoid attendance at every one of the interminable AGO conventions which demanded attention at least twice a year, but as a major staff member at national headquarters he could not always pull that off. So, whenever he and I had to attend a convention, John and Rollin developed the pattern of going out together. One of the movies they saw featured a young actor who was then in his prime and currently popular, I think his name was Sam Elliot. Anyway, he was flirting with a girl on screen when Rollin, in full voice, offered another of his unfiltered commentaries on life. John reported an audience reaction similar to that we'd experienced in the restaurant.

Meanwhile Tony and I were having yet another AGO convention experience, which traditionally involved a fair amount of drinking. This time, in St. Louis, we fell in with a group because it included Tony's friend John Obetz who was also on the program as a recitalist. I remember the evening before Obetz's mid-morning performance, first with some surprise that he drank as he usually did, with a performance just a few hours away, and then astonishment that he pushed on well past midnight when I finally gave up and retired to my room next door. I could not tell you if he played well the next morning because my own sensory equipment was not yet liberated from the excess of the previous evening, but there he was on schedule at the keyboards playing what sounded to me to be the program he was scheduled to perform.

John Obetz was one of the many bigger than life characters in the AGO and John (Rose) and I hosted him in Newark a couple of times when he performed on John's organ series at Sacred Heart Cathedral. He stands out in my memory largely for a story he told on himself. When his son was old enough to put three and three together, he found his parents at home one day and asked them, "Are you guys gay?" The boy's mother volunteered, "Well, **I'M** not."

Okay, that brings us squarely to a quick discussion which I don't think can be avoided in this memoir, although I don't think it deserves to be highlighted either.

Organists & Me

Church music, and maybe church organists in particular, was one of those professions in which one was not surprised if the next guy in the pew were gay. He wasn't always, to be sure, but one had to be careful not to bet too much money against the possibility. Why this should be the case got discussed upon occasion, but no one had any theories which made particular sense. A lot of organists were toy train (and real train) enthusiasts as well, and some people said that was another group which had more than its fair share of gay men. Someday, if I get the chance, maybe I'll ask St. Peter about it.

For understandable reasons the AGO had never compiled statistics on the sexual orientation of its membership; probably mostly because it liked to take a fairly modest stance on most things and didn't want to appear to be bragging about its embarrassment of riches. Probably also because it might have been regarded as unseemly to hog so much of the gay talent for itself when some other professions were left largely wanting.

So I can't give you a bottom line hard number on this matter, but I can safely report that on the eleventh day of creation when God sat down to allot gay men to the various identifiable occupational groups He was planning, He was in a very generous mood toward the organists.

[*A serious comment I'd like to insert: While I don't advocate dishonesty or cover-ups, I think subjects like this should be handled discreetly because people's lives and reputations are at stake and no one should be branded as "different" by a broad brush used indiscriminately. Not all organists are gay. And therefore, being an organist does not automatically mean one is gay.*

One of only two times I've been enraged by my faithful companion The New York Times *was when an article was published sometime in the seventies or eighties, I think, which stated flatly that organists tended to be gay, but offered no actual statistics or medical backup. This was written by a silly young woman who flirted around our organist ranks and somehow conned the* NYT *into buying one of her freelance articles to which it then failed to provide proper editorial supervision. My concern was for the young people coming up in the organist field who could, as a result, be blackballed for a needed church music job merely by the suggestion that they were probably gay. I've rarely seen the* NYT *print anything that irresponsible before or since.*]

All of this having been said, however, it can be safely observed that the after-hours scene at any AGO convention in my day always tended to evoke a gay bar. Perhaps the straight organists just had enough common sense to go to bed on time and didn't want to attend the next day's first event with a hangover. Still, I can honestly note that I've known convention regulars who started out bringing wives along, but then gradually transitioned to boyfriends. Folklore on the street has it that among the other professions top-heavy with gays is that of the clergy, which my own experience does not contradict. If true, it makes for a potentially interesting pairing in the chancel between the priest/pastor and the organist/choirmaster. Maybe it also helps to explain the sense of rivalry between these chancel figures which in my day was very frequently in evidence.

Probably I should note again here that I'm writing mostly about the second half of the 20th century and the early part of the 21st, and so should acknowledge that the social climate has gotten much better for the LGBTQ community by now, although ironically the church scene upon which so many organists depend for jobs seems to be declining in proportion.

One additional aspect of the organ's effect on personalities can also be noted in passing—the strange way that non-organists can become addicted to the instrument in substantial ways without ever being musicians themselves, or at least without ever being organists themselves. I'm a good example myself, and earlier I've mentioned Tony Baglivi, longtime TAO editor, in that light. So far as I can detect, the legendary agent for organists Lillian Murtagh was not herself an organist. Neither of the two Executive Directors of the AGO whose careers have paralleled mine were organists, and the first of these two has gone on after retirement from the AGO to head up yet another organ focused organization. My agency partner Ray Albright is another example of a non-organist who, after the agency was sold, still had not had enough organ in his life and so he became a builder of the intoxicating contraptions.

The last example I'll name is a person I've been looking for an excuse to slip into this book anyway, The Most Rev. John J. O'Hara, Auxiliary (Catholic) Bishop of New York. For as long as I've known John, which dates back to immediately after his college days, he has been one of the greatest friends of the organ on the scene, a strong supporter of performers and possessed of a wealth of knowledge on the art form and its history. From what I can gather even now he is a legendary figure in the circles of New York area organists who benefit frequently from his advice and encouragement. He can hold forth on famous organists and organs and organ literature for hours at a time from memory. Yet, like me, if you sat him down in front of an organ console, the instrument would need to remain silent.

So personalities in the realm of the organ include far more key figures than simply organists themselves. The instrument evidently has a way of capturing people of many stripes, and holding them tight.

13 Conventions

Attending an AGO convention was always a little like going to an opera matinee at the Met. There was always a scattering of young people around, clinging to each other in self-protective little knots. But mostly one was swallowed up in a sea of gray hair, or no hair at all for that matter. My own transition from a member of the minority young to the majority whatever-hair-is-left-is-gray took a great many conventions to accomplish; so many that the host cycle not only had run though the country's major cities, but was well into its second round (and in some cases even a third round, especially if one counted both national and regional conventions).

All these conventions provided a collective great tapestry of fine (or at least good) performers and a fair display of the organ's literature. But in truth I can't easily sort them out as individual units anymore; they live in memory as an undivided unit—that great AGO convention in the sky. Programs had a pattern that varied little from one convention to the next. The people attending didn't vary all that much either, they just kept coming back for the next round and aging in the process. The after-hours drinking had to have involved lots of different companions over all those years, but my remaining mental picture is a gloss of hotel bars which belong in Boston just as comfortably as Atlanta or San Francisco. An AGO convention was a multiple birth, a quintuplet or whatever word carries on from there.

Certainly there were highlights along the way. There was the convention at which I offered "Houli fan" coffee mugs at our booth and got sick of the parade of little old ladies stopping to ask "What's a 'Houli'?" I finally threw a big fake smile at one of them and said, "Congratulations, you've just said the magic phrase," and gave her a free CD as her prize. Then I had to endure the rest of the convention with lines of little old women toddling up to our booth and shouting, "'What's a 'Houli?' Give me my free CD."

Then there was the convention where we accidently treated lots of people to an unintended lunch. To celebrate a significant agency anniversary, probably our 20th or 25th, memory is a bit rusty on the exact details, I decided to stage a reception. Conventions were the only time our presenters (customers) and artists were together in significant numbers, so the setting was an obvious choice. The event was conceived as a late afternoon affair of wine and *hors d'oeuvres*, a sort of happy hour before

Conventions

dinner. Finding a workable time in the crowded convention schedule, however, forced us to a late morning spot, so we became a prelude to lunch rather than dinner.

Hotel rules forced any food and drink served to be purchased directly from the hotel, so this was a catered affair and rather expensive to host. People circulated and seemed to be enjoying themselves, and I noticed that they seemed to linger much longer that I had expected. Shouldn't they be going off for lunch before the next scheduled convention event? So I ordered more supplies from the hotel kitchen. Then from our balcony perch I noticed on the main floor below a couple who had just left our reception. They paused to compare notes, presumably about where to grab a quick lunch. But then they turned around and came back upstairs and were soon enjoying our hospitality again. It finally dawned on me that these very practical and pragmatic organists were simply allowing PTCA to provide their lunch for the day.

Why were there so many AGO conventions (nationals, regionals, midwinter conclaves, ICOs, etc.)? There were the noble reasons of fellowship, education, etc., but there was also a slightly less magnanimous, more self-serving motivation. Conventions made money, and in capitalistic America even an organization which thought it might be doing the work of the Lord wanted as much money as it could get, although for purely lofty reasons, of course. Yes, conventions made money—until Detroit. That Detroit national convention (the first there, I think, but I wasn't doing a good job of keeping track) brought the AGO to its loss of economic innocence. Henceforth the national office took a careful guiding hand in the planning and budgeting for any convention with an AGO title.

I sometimes felt the AGO was pushing its members too hard financially by these seemingly endless conventions. It was expensive to fly across the country and live in a hotel for a week, and AGO members were for the most part church musicians who could not afford to live very high on the hog. When I started to attend them, beginning in 1970, some of the regionals headquartered themselves on college campuses and thus offered dorm room accommodations. That feet-on-the-ground approach was gasping its last, however, and hotels soon became the *de rigueur* playgrounds of the AGO conventioneers.

This was a more comfortable arrangement, to be sure, but I think it had the unintended consequence of limiting the number of members who could attend. Gradually only musicians from churches large enough to provide them with expense accounts or "educational" allowances were showing up, joined by the academics with similar perks. For the average church organist without such an advantage, a convention week cost a significant part of one's annual budget. These people often had to choose between an AGO convention and any other sort of annual vacation, but there were always those in attendance for whom the AGO convention was the great highlight and extravagance of the year. That sometimes bothered me, but I was only a sort of honorary member of the clan and probably my fever level for being with other organ-types was lower than that of most of the others.

It bothered me also, however, because I was investing large sums of money in these conventions (travel, hotel, meals and registration for agency staff, booth rental, and advertising) and for me and the other exhibition hall denizens it was important to have as large a convention attendance as possible. (Many convention attendees did not even get around to the exhibition room until the final hour when exhibitors had begun to dismantle their booths, and presumably some did not get around to it at all.)

Why the national organization had previously left local chapters to host AGO conventions with total independence and freedom had long puzzled and frustrated me. Whatever the local host committee planned or scheduled had the implied imprimatur of the national organization. I was in the business of promoting the careers of specific performers and therefore sensitive to the promotional advantage inherited by any performer invited to be on an AGO convention program. The effect was an apparent endorsement of those particular artists as the best in the field of the day, and the invitation therefore gave them a big leg up in getting further bookings. AGO conventions, in short, functioned as showcases for specific performers, but not for others who were equally (or even more) talented. The national organization never did anything to ease that problem (such as establishing a national committee to select convention artists, or stipulating a limit on how many conventions in a row a specific artist could be featured), but it did have to grow up and start paying more attention to the economic realities and jeopardies of convention hosting.

The artists invited to perform at conventions continued, as in the past, to be chosen entirely by a program sub-committee of a local AGO chapter's convention hosting committee. This meant, in effect, that every other year one individual, the program committee chairman, got to decide independently which artists would get a national spotlight and the implied status of the best performers the country had to offer. Maybe I was the only one who felt this was a defect in the system (although I have no doubt that my fellow agents were also bothered when performers they did not represent got the implied endorsement of the national organization, sometimes the same established artists repeatedly at convention after convention which became a roadblock for younger talent to emerge).

There was a way around the problem, and as usual in life, even life in the AGO, it involved money. I served on three regional AGO convention hosting committees for my local chapter (Greater Hartford), the first of which went down in AGO history as the only committee to have its convention yanked and given to another chapter (because the regional AGO chairperson got into a fight with the program committee chairman over a vocal ensemble he wanted to feature). The second committee fared much better and actually got to host a convention which set new standards of success, in both attendance and artistic quality, for AGO regionals.

The chairman assigned me to "exhibits" because I was the only chapter member with actual experience running a booth at national and regional AGO conventions—lots and lots of such experience. My real interest was in constructing the program, however. I understood why I, a business representative for many organist performers, would be an inappropriate choice to head the programming committee, or even to sit on it. I was eminently qualified, however, having attended more organ performances and having heard more individual organists perform than anyone else in my chapter, by far. But the pool of experience I represented did not extend very broadly in chapter membership. So we ended up with a program chairman who, though a good musician and a nice guy, had never attended an AGO convention in his life—and now suddenly found himself in charge of deciding almost everything pertinent about our convention including which artists would perform.

Since then I've observed this same circumstance and attitude at work in the very similar dynamics of operating an organ performance competition (this one the ASOFH). I was the only member of the board of directors of the competition to have attended several seasons each of some of the biggest international organ performance competitions, but when I pointed out that none of them did some of the controversial things we were doing, someone brushed away my objection on the basis that we could do whatever we wanted to. While true, this approach prevented us from benefitting from the experience of organizations much older and much more prestigious than ours. Perhaps there was something about organists which made them prefer to reinvent the wheel, or to remain happily isolated from anyone else's successful accomplishments and methods.

The regional AGO convention committee I was working on was operating only a little more than two years before our slated convention, and there was just enough time to send the program committee chairman to attend that year's AGO regional. After that, at last, we had a 'veteran' AGO convention goer at the head of our program committee, albeit with only one (I thought) dismal and ill-attended such convention under his belt (I was there too, as usual, with an exhibition booth).

Our program committee came up with what to my eyes was the typical non-exciting list of performers, all of whom had either performed at several conventions previously or had never been heard of by anyone beyond the committee member who probably had nominated them because of friendship.

Paul Jacobs was on my agency roster of artists then and, although still young, already had a sterling national reputation head and shoulders above anyone our program committee had drug out on their unsurprising list of performers. Paul's name was soaring in popularity at that point, which gave me the perfect opportunity to cut across the nonsense and get a recognized artist of world-caliber talent installed as our convention headliner. The simple trick was to dangle money, or in this case, to arrange for Paul's fee to be paid as a gift to the chapter so it would not have to be part of the convention budget.

I then managed to get Paul a big feature article in our local newspaper's Sunday arts section, complete with a full page color cover photo. This helped ensure that Paul's performance was an unqualified success, and brought so much attention to our convention that it gathered in a standing-room-only audience several times larger than the number registered to attend the convention itself. Everyone was thrilled, including the program chairman and his committee who gladly took their share of credit for our coup.

AGO conventions were not the only such duty to befall an agent for musical performers, at least if the agent represented anyone beyond organists, as I did. My AGO oriented colleagues stuck strictly to the organ field, which had its own perfectly logical rationale. Performing organists were bound by instruments which were decidedly not portable, and most of their potential performance instruments, at least at that time, were to be found in churches and colleges rather than concert halls. Therefore organ performance as an art form constituted a separate world from the concert scene in general—separate venues, separate performers, separate presenters. It was perfectly natural for an agent to have both feet on one side of the divide or the other. Why I wanted to break that mold may say something about me which even I don't understand, but I can say with some deserved pride that I did it successfully and for a number of years.

Perhaps I should reveal a dark secret at this point. The curmudgeonly stance I've taken in talking about AGO conventions is partially a charade. While they were a relentless and obligatory part of my calendar, and a constant interruption to the real work of the agency—I actually loved them and for the most part anticipated each one with pleasure. Lots of organists seemed to use AGO conventions as a vacation (or at least as a busman's holiday) and I probably slipped a little into that category myself, but please don't tell on me. I'd prefer to retain my self-sacrificial image of all work and no play.

Conventions

The truth is that AGO conventions for me were a mixed bag. They got my colleagues out of the organ loft and me out of the office, and gave each of us a legitimate professional cover to rationalize the expense of cash and time required. And I suppose it's also fair to say that some residual benefits showed up at income tax time.

14 AGO Conventions as Trade Shows

From the beginning of my career as an agent I had utilized AGO conventions as trade shows for the promotion of my concert artists, an innovation my friend and colleague Karen McFarlane left to me alone. Some of the younger agents along the way dipped their toes in this idea as well, following my example, but I can't remember any who lasted more than a couple of conventions in the attempt.

Our first utilization of an AGO convention as a trade show opportunity was at the very first AGO convention I attended, in 1970 in Westchester County NY. In terms of the parallel history of Karen's and my agencies, I believe this might have been before she started her first business, but those very early years are a bit hazy by now. At any rate, the agency which became PTCA had been advertising for a time (three years or so) in *MUSIC*, the official AGO journal (pre-TAO), and I decided it was time to expand into live promotion at AGO conventions.

We rented our first exhibition space at an AGO gathering, just a simple table upon which to spread some of our fledgling literature for pick up. Whether to stay close to the table during exhibition hours, or be off meeting people in other ways instead, was one of the first questions I had to answer. As I recall we (myself and most of our early small roster of artists) did spend a lot of time in the small exhibition room but maybe not quite in the way we expected would be the case. Traffic in the room was a great deal lighter than my expectations, or hopes, would have pictured, and we fell in with an older guy who was there to man the exhibit for his organ-building firm, one of the Odell men probably in the middle generation of that firm's owners. He was good company and we spent hours listening to his stories and grateful to have someone to talk with, but at the same time frustrated that so few conventioneers were coming through the exhibition space. I guess stubbornness may be a significant component of my personality, however, because despite the slow beginning we kept at this "trade show" approach to AGO conventions for decades to come.

Yes, we were inventing the wheel, but two years later at the 1972 national AGO convention in Dallas we stayed with the task and greatly expanded the concept. This time we rented an entire room on our own. At subsequent conventions I would decide that the better location was inside the main exhibition room with most of the other exhibitors in order to gain optimum traffic flow. Luckily, however, the hotel layout in Dallas placed our room at the top of the escalators and just outside the entrance to the main exhibition room, so we weren't at too much of a disadvantage.

The concept at this first of our two Dallas national AGO conventions was to make our artists available for personal meeting and conversation with conventioneers. Our roster was, understandably for that time in the agency's history, composed of young organists not very much known yet as performers. So we had carts of coffee and pastries catered to our room by the hotel, hoping to attract folks either entering or leaving the main hall—maybe even using our set-up as a quick breakfast substitute. I organized the agency's artists so that each had exhibition room "duty" at some specified time of day so that one of them would always be present to chat with our visiting coffee drinkers. For some reason I recall now the pain this caused Hap (Dr. Frank) Speller (University of Texas faculty) who complied but was very shy of meeting people and spent most of this 'meet and greet' time glued to his chair.

At each convention we tried to make some kind of concept advance which would make our booth (usually a double, sometimes a triple booth) increasingly interesting and less stereotypical. At one I decided to try to paint our artists in larger terms than merely musicians to give them a fuller personality profile. We rented several monitors which could show photo images in rotation for several seconds per image, and invited the artists to send us color slides of themselves not only at organ consoles but outdoors, at their hobbies, or anything which might be interesting or attractive. Everyone on the roster cooperated except the then organ professor on the Indiana University faculty who lectured me that trying these sorts of gimmicks was pointless and that any responsible way to promote organists had been invented a long time ago and I should stop trying to go outside the box. I didn't follow his advice, and at every convention we tried to add something which would make our booth(s) more appealing and less stereotypical.

Representing performers other than organists, however, meant that AGO conventions were no longer adequate on their own as trade shows.

Our agency mounted exhibition space at a number of "secular" (non-AGO) musical trade shows in New York for a long number of years, for the most part the annual event sponsored by the Association of Performing Arts Presenters and its predecessor organization. These events were staged in the bleak mid-winter, which in Manhattan with icy winds whipping through tunnels of skyscrapers could be bleak indeed. While I always tried to promote my organist artists as well, the presenters who attended these shows really never had the capacity to respond because they lacked an instrument, and to bring in an electronic organ for a particular event added enough cost to make it a risky commitment, especially in the minds of presenters who did not know the organ or have any kind of personal connection with it or affection for it. So these trade shows yielded results only for our non-organist side of the roster, although they did greatly help in our booking of English choirs, so church music did collect some of the benefits.

For whatever reason notwithstanding, our super-star (among AGO types at the time) organist Gillian Weir was interested enough to want to see the APAP show floor while on a New York visit. I was able to get her a pass by some mechanism or other, but her husband, the sometime pipe organ builder and sometime electronic organ builder Larry Phelps, needed one as well. My (then future) husband John Rose was in New York for the show with me as usual and registered at the event through the agency. He lent his badge to Larry as a favor for the afternoon.

Phelps was at the time a big proponent of digital electronic organs, and John had been representing another brand on the side for a bit of extra income. I remember watching Larry stare at his borrowed badge with some dejection and saying, "No one is going to believe I'm an analogue man." Of course, at the moment we were in a world where no one was going to know or care what the ding-dong he was even talking about, or for that matter who in the world was Lawrence Phelps or John Rose, or even Gillian Weir.

AGO conventions were always a double-edged sword for me. I did look forward to seeing all the regulars every year, but I also hated having to be away from home just at that particular time of year. I was for quite a time an enthusiast of day-lilies and had amassed quite a large and varied collection. The conventions always were scheduled just at the point my day-lilies reached their peak, and I hated being away at the very week they were doing their star-turn.

The timing of AGO conventions also killed July Fourth celebrations at home. Having grown up in a small Iowa town in the middle of the 20th century, the Fourth of July (we never called it "Independence Day" in Winterset) was sacred on many levels, but it was always a day one wanted to be at home for the family picnic, the parade, and the fire-works. The AGO could get better hotel rates over this holiday, and July Fourth not being a particularly churchy event, I guess it was calculated that we'd all be perfectly happy to make our patriotism portable for the much more important glory of the organ, or at least for church music. I spent many a Fourth of July morning out buying American flags with which to decorate the agency convention booth in time for its evening run, and wondering why I seemed to be almost the only convention booth holder with that concern.

AGO Conventions as Trade Shows

In all I attended and mounted an exhibition booth at a minimum of 67 such conventions and trade shows, well over a full year's worth of time cut from my lifetime, away from home and dogs, and sometimes family (much of the time John and Ray were at the conventions enjoying themselves along with me). And in terms of budget and sanity, well over a full year living out of a suitcase in a hotel room. This included eight repeat cities for AGO conventions and two cities with triple AGO runs, plus at least 13 general music trade shows in New York City and one in Europe. All of those hotels and all of that drinking should have cured me of wanting to travel in retirement, but in that department I turned out to be a slow learner.

15 Competitions for Organ Performance

By the time young organists reach the stage of wanting to enter a performance competition they usually have something to say artistically, and are at least beginning to develop musical personalities and some stage presence. Audiences care about those aspects. Judges, on the other hand, are required to care about correct notes and stylistic appropriateness. It's not much of a surprise that the audience prize (when there is one) sometimes goes to a competitor other than the official winner, or that sometimes the actual winner has more difficulty establishing a performance career than does a peer who didn't place as high on the judges' ballots.

And the judges are not always impartial or fair, although I'm sure most of them want and try to be and, certainly, think they are. At one of the Dallas competitions I sat at table with a group of judges after the event and heard the Swiss organist Guy Bovet brag that he had knocked one competitor completely out of the running because of something Bovet did not like about the player's Bach. It was a one-to-ten scoring ballot, so all he had to do was give the young organist a 'ten' (the scale was one=best; ten=worst) on his Bach line when probably a 'three' or 'four' would have sufficiently made the point and reflected reality. This effectively skewed the system and totally eliminated the particular competitor regardless of the quality of his non-Bach work.

I've never been sure that performance competitions always yielded the most worthy performer as the winner. But be that as it may, young performers flocked to such competitions, and heaven knows there were a lot of them to flock to. There seemed to be many score of such competitions offered by individual churches and individual AGO chapters, all with rather modest prizes and modest prestige attached. These minor competitions came and went with athletic frequency, but there was at least one which deserved credit for staying power; it was sponsored by First Presbyterian Church in Fort Wayne IN.

There were also a few which offered far greater prestige and a nice fat purse. These "international" competitions, as they always styled themselves, became a distinguishing mark for the two major organist agencies. PTCA represented the top winners (offered as part of the prize) of the Chartres International Organ Competition in France, the St. Albans International

Competitions for Organ Performance

Competition in England, both with long standing histories under their belts, and the Dallas International Organ Competition in Texas for the entire time of its several year run. Just before my retirement I agreed to link also with the Longwood International Competition in Pennsylvania which offers the highest monetary prize of any of them. Charles was in place as head of the agency by the time the second of these Longwood winners was announced.

McFarlane worked with two major competitions in a similar manner (if there were more I'm not omitting mention of them out of spite, but sheerly out the treachery of a retired guy's memory). The AGO national organ performance competition took place biennially at AGO national conventions. I recall hearing from the beginning that Karen's involvement was because of funding that Lillian Murtagh had left for the prize, but that's second hand information which may be weak in some details. The second major competition that I recall McFarlane was involved with was the Canadian International Organ Competition. Their agency then, for a set period, represented the winners of those competitions as did we the winners of our competitions. For both agencies this representation was guaranteed only until the winner had a successor, but in some cases both agencies then added such winners to their regular on-going rosters.

There is another organ performance competition in the U.S. now attempting to consolidate a place in the top tier, The Albert Schweitzer Organ Festival Hartford. I've worked for several years as a member of the board and vice president to further the contribution this competition makes, and in return that lets me stretch the truth just a tiny bit. I really wanted to postpone retirement from the agency until the fifty year mark, but Charles Miller's schedule would not allow him to take over the agency later than my 48th year anniversary. Since I've continued to work in the organ performance field long past what would have been my 50th anniversary at the agency, I allow myself to speak of my 'half-century' in the field, and to do it without undue guilt. Since so many folks see the AGO as a quasi-religious organization anyway, I'll accept an indulgence on my arithmetic, and count my service to the competition as a continuation of my work at PTCA.

ASOFH began well over two decades before this writing and for long years was a labor of love of just one man, the late David Spicer. As such it picked up along the way a number of his quirks and acquired a sort of evangelical religious overlay. Because he was an especially gifted hymn player, the competition also added a hymn playing competition which is still rare (maybe even unique) among other of the organ performance competitions I've observed in Europe or at home. Whenever I made noises questioning why a hymn competition or a religious service (religious in appearance anyway, during the early years) were valid features of an organ playing competition, I was slapped down by some of the members of the board who had been part of David Spicer's support group who assured me that our young competitors would have to become church organists whether they liked it or not, and that none of them would stand a snowball's chance of being just a concert organist. Actually one of them, Christopher Houlihan, did in fact earn his entire living from performing for a number of years, until he was offered an endowed position at his alma mater. And another, Paul Jacobs, never held a church music job after grad school (although he occasionally substituted as a favor to a friend or institution).

As you may have guessed from reading this so far, my involvement and investment was purely on a secular level, and I believed the organ deserved to be treated as a legitimate musical instrument rather than a kind of appendage to organized religion.

We made some progress in letting this competition evolve in ways I believe are healthy. The quasi-religious Evangelical-feeling opening service (it was called a 'concert' despite prayers, hymns, religious choral anthems, and inspired oratory) has been replaced with an Evensong which at least does not try to disguise what it really is (although I see it as a further step into an unfortunate ambiguity for the festival). The hymn playing part of the competition is no longer mandatory. If I were king of the world I'd have made some further changes, but I'm not, and I'm sure there are ASFOH fellow board members who get on their knees every night to give thanks that I'm not.

When David Spicer ran into resistance to hosting this competition/festival from his increasingly 'conservative' parish, he set the wheels in motion to move ASOF (the "H" was added later) to Trinity College, with its exceptionally fine Austin organ. And not at all that long later when his health was sending him unhappy signals, he pulled all the right strings to set up the organization as a legal non-profit entity with a board of strong community leaders headed by Bob Bausmith, still our president. John and I, by then both board members, recruited John's former student Vaughn Mauren as a new board member, and he was later elected to replace David Spicer as Artistic Director after Spicer's death.

Anyway, I can report that from humble and difficult origins a determined one man effort has turned into an increasingly major U.S. organ performance competition steeled to surviving and flourishing for the long haul. It takes place annually (our 2020 edition was technically postponed, but was thereby effectively cancelled because of the pandemic), unlike any other major organ performance competition I know of in the U.S., or anywhere else for that matter, and also unlike any other I know of, it serves

Competitions for Organ Performance

both high school aged organists and university aged organists on alternate years.

Well before I was involved in the organization, this competition had propelled some of the finest organists my agency had the honor to represent into the beginning of prominence: Paul Jacobs, Christopher Houlihan, David Enlow, and Simon Thomas Jacobs. Ironically perhaps, despite my being assured by fellow board members that no organist could exist in a secular setting, two of these artists, Jacobs and Houlihan, as mentioned above, have both proven that idea false. Both flourish now in academic settings and both are major artists of the organ standing independently as a legitimate concert instrument (even though that's not the same thing as saying they don't perform in churches).

The Achilles heel of the ASOFH organ performance competition, in my view, is that it clings to the same confusion I see in the AGO itself; the question of whether it is a religious organization or not? Most of my colleagues don't seem to want to acknowledge that such confusion exists, and if they do see it at all they prefer to look at it as the innocent by-product of so many organists working as church musicians. I see it as a quite willful and deliberate confusion—organists really **want** their organizations to be quasi-religious in nature and practice; it's where they feel at home. This is a self-described performance competition for organists which now places its winner's recital in the same program package as a religious service conducted by ordained clergy—if one wants to hear the winner perform, one has to attend a full-blown Evensong or make a public display of leaving before Evensong begins. That's not just tolerating the confusion, it's institutionalizing it.

Our agency garnered some other fine performers from the winners of other competitions as well, as noted in the appendices. This sometimes got a little sticky when the winner already had ties to one of the agencies, but the competition was offering winners to a different agency. For us the most stark example came at a Chartres competition when the winner was already on the McFarlane roster. I had shelled out, as usual, a lot of money for me and my top assistant to be in Chartres for the event in a show of support and solidarity, and to be able to speak immediately with the next winner as we had done previously. Well, this time it was a pretty awkward situation, so what to do? We talked with the winner, as we really had to do, and offered him the spot on our roster he had just won without really expecting that he'd be interested. As I intuited, he wasn't. He was perfectly happy to stay with McFarlane, as indeed was the rational thing for him to do, and as even I recognized.

My idea of a solution to this sort of situation was to suggest to the competition that the rules should exclude from eligibility anyone who was already represented by a major organists' agency. The competition manager reacted with horror to that idea. Their system used only age as a determining factor for eligibility, and since the French were unquestionably correct in all their assumptions and orientations, it would be totally and absolutely impossible to add such a restriction. As you might guess, I decided to suspend the practice of a couple of us attending the Chartres competition in person, thereby saving the agency a wad of hard-to-come-by cash every second year.

John McElliott didn't seem very pleased that we'd even perfunctorily offered a roster place to the winner, despite our obligation to the competition to do so. He lectured me about the time Clive Driskill-Smith had won a competition in Canada to which John's agency provided an agency roster spot to the winner. But I had just admitted Clive to our roster before that competition win, after some long and strong lobbying on his behalf by Ralph Allwood of Eton College. The details of what had happened, and in what sequence are somewhat murky for me by now, but John McElliott evidently felt he should have first dibs on Clive.

I was in Europe on business, as was frequently the case, so Clive had easy access to talking with me directly. He and his uncle flew to Paris from London and we talked at my hotel for a couple of hours, after which he decided to remain on our roster rather than move over to McFarlane as part of the competition prize. My memory does not convict me of stealing from McElliott, but I'm pretty sure he was seeing the situation differently, or at least so he grumbled.

After my retirement, John McElliott and Charles Miller were thrown into a similar bind. Charles had recently admitted an American performer and was already featuring him in agency advertising. Then the young organist entered the Canadian CIOC competition and won. John McElliott was now in exactly the same position I'd been in much earlier in France. He, of course, extended an invitation to the winner because he had an agreement with the competition to do so. The shoe was on the other foot.

In this case Charles played the gentleman, and released the young organist from his contract with PTCA, making him free to move over to McFarlane. Charles certainly did not have to do this—a contract is a contract, even in the religiously besotted circles of organists. I think that self-sacrificing move by Charles was far more professionally accommodating, however, than McElliott had been with the Chartres winner, and most probably more professionally accommodating than I had been with Clive, although I still can't remember the fine points and sequence of that episode in clear detail.

It still seems to me that if these competitions want to beef up their prizes with offers of automatic agency representation, they have some obligation to prevent these sorts of conflicts. On this, I have little doubt, John McElliott and I are on the same page. Each competition has all kinds of rules governing eligibility, so if they want to dangle representation by a major agency as part of the prize, it is only logical that entrants should not already be represented by a major agency. Besides, the competitions are supposed to be for emerging artists, and major representation is a sign that the organist has already launched on a professional performance career. The competitions should belong to those who really need the help of taking first steps, rather than just an additional feather in the cap of someone already launched on a performance career.

So were some of the tangles we organist agents could get ourselves tied up in, and so the lingering sense of competition which colored our relationships. Anyway, both PTCA and McFarlane made significant contributions to the field through these competition prizes, and encouraging and supporting young talent was a strongly felt part of the mission of both agencies.

This pattern of a major agency contract being part of the top prize in an organ performance competition was another of my innovations (at least in so far as competitions beyond that of the national AGO convention). It began with the Philadelphia session of the International Congress of Organists when I was invited to participate in the prize. The host committee envisioned a sort of 'victory lap' tour of pre-arranged and fee-paying recitals for the competition winner to walk into without delay, and asked me to set one up. Having worked daily with the presenters our field had to offer, however, I knew very few would sign up to present a player they could have no advance idea about. So I suggested instead that the agency offer a roster membership to the winning artist on a limited term basis. This way we could take advantage of the prestige of the win as an inducement to presenters, and indeed within a few months the winner, David Hurd, did get his victory lap of several fee-paying performances.

David became a quick audience and presenter favorite and at the end of whatever period had been agreed to, we were delighted to offer him an ongoing place on our roster of artists; a place he then held for the decades of my remaining time at the agency helm, and holds still under Charles, my successor.

16 Towerhill Recordings

For some years PTCA had another distinction among agencies for organists: its own record label.

At one of John Rose's early performances in Los Angeles, a young man came bounding up to him at the reception line and introduced himself; Michael Nemo, a recording engineer for several of the big Hollywood recording studios, the engineer for a number of currently high-riding pop singers, and another of the incurable organ enthusiasts who populated our scene. He had heard something in John's performing which set off an excitement he'd not experienced before. Michael's organ affliction had begun when he was a teenager attending Hollywood High School, which had its own Skinner pipe organ and a crew of boys who loved to play it and tinker with it. Michael asked John if he'd be willing to record for him and volunteered to set up his own label for releases if the answer was 'yes,' which of course it was.

Michael Nemo (right) with John Rose.

In due course Michael and John were working together in California, then in New Jersey, and then in Connecticut. Michael managed to sell some of the results to established labels (which gave John the thrill of accidently discovering his first album in several New York record stores), but eventually decided the best course would be to establish the new label he had at first envisioned. He had earlier in his career owned a large mansion in Los Angeles, high on Mullholland Drive, to which he had added a big tower of his own design. The project had nearly bankrupted him, but it still had a place in his heart and thus "Towerhill Recordings" was born.

Towerhill Recordings

Among the LPs and CDs issued of John's playing was a highly acclaimed series called "The French Romantics" which focused on the symphonic school organ composers such as Vierne, Widor, Guilmant, Franck, etc. The most stir, however, was probably caused by a single album they recorded at the Roman Catholic cathedral in Hartford. A potentially block-buster film had just been released by one of the Hollywood studios to which Michael maintained his ties, a little flick named "Star Wars." The popular Boston Pops director John Williams had written the musical score and Michael had the unorthodox idea of recording an organ version of the film score.

Michael obtained the rights to transcribe the Williams movie score for organ and the task was assigned to Robert Edward Smith, working in Newark. John had to go to the Greyhound bus station in Hartford every day to collect Robert's newest work before editing it and giving it the final adaptation to the organ. With the transcription finally in hand, Michael and John set up a studio in the cathedral. Recording took place at night, as was frequently necessary in a busy venue where daytime activity brought in all kinds of extraneous sounds. One early morning the tape revealed an unexpected sound of sirens which was explained only when John and Michael closed shop and emerged into the murky dawn. John's car was not parked on the street where it had been left the evening before. A call to the police from a street pay phone revealed that it had been smashed by a drunk driver, and towed to a police lot.

The end product of these recording sessions caused a stir in organ circles. Scott Cantrell wrote in a TAO review that "This may be the most exciting organ recording I've ever heard." Later Peter Richard Conte told John that this "Star Wars" album had opened his eyes to the endless possibilities of using the organ in transcription, and that it played a role in his rise to become organist of the great Wanamaker instrument in Philadelphia. A number of other organists, however, predictably collected their self-righteousness and sneered that John was some kind of traitor to the cause of organ purity—a movie score based on science fiction? The nerve!

Organists & Me

After one such recording visit I went to the airport with Michael on his way back to California with some of the 'French Romantics' tapes. The security guards were immediately suspicious of these heavy-duty professional reels of wide tape housed in round metal containers, and although we were still many years away from the post 9/11 airport security everyone faces today, the guards insisted that every container be opened and every tape at least partially unwound.

Meanwhile, pizza delivery boys carrying closed boxes of nearly identical dimensions were waved through the check-point without even one box being opened. I guess these crack government agents could be sure those boxes were perfectly safe because, after all, they were labeled "pizza" right on the cardboard.

This was all during the time the "gay plague" was still raging and had started to mow down some worthy names among our AGO ranks. Michael lived in free-partying Hollywood and was a secular soul unbound by Sunday School rules and regulations. We took note when his across-the-street neighbor, a guy we knew from visits to Hollywood, died of HIV/AIDS. I think we didn't really stop to worry about Michael, our somewhat up-tight Eastern lives being so different in style than his, but we should have. In due course he fell with the others who would be memorialized on the huge AIDS Quilts.

Michael left to John all of his professional recording equipment, and a big semi-trailer arrived in front of our Harford house one day to disgorge it. Ray, our agency partner and housemate, was a trained electrical engineer for whom nothing was much of a mystery and nothing much was impossible, so we had a successor recording engineer and decided we'd continue the Towerhill label as a tribute to Michael Nemo and as a service to the agency roster members who were always looking for opportunities in the recording field.

This worked well for a time, and for a couple of years we had a national distributor, very difficult to find even back then. But soon enough it became obvious that it wasn't really possible to run several demanding businesses under one corporation and without a big staff; and it also became obvious that we were working Ray too hard by adding recording engineer, graphic cover designer, and distribution manager to his many other indispensable jobs within the company.

During the Towerhill period, however, we did release several CDs by other of our organists, including the debut disc by Christopher Houlihan who has now gone on to other national recording labels. Our pianists, especially Paul Bisaccia, took good advantage of the option as well, and the label probably became top-heavy in that genre. There was also a scattering of other releases, including one CD by The Texas Boys Choir which had won two Grammy Awards for previous recordings on major labels.

Towerhill Records, during Michael Nemo's day, came close to opening a new era for CD albums. With his roots and connections in the Hollywood entertainment industry, he was aware of investigations as to whether code spaces between movements could be used for something beyond unheard instructions to the CD player. He managed to take one of John's 'French Romantics' albums and insert a string of cartoonish and photo illustrations into to previously unused digital space, so that with the right equipment one could both hear, and see, the CD.

Although others tried to make a viable thing out of this technology as well, the idea ultimately didn't go very far as a commercial success. The problem was that special equipment was required to read the graphics, whereas these same compact discs worked perfectly as well as did standard CDs on standard CD players. The extra consumer expense involved ultimately doomed the idea. We are, however, left with a few remaining discs marked distinctively "Compact Disc Digital Audio Graphics" as a souvenir of what might have been—most of our supply of them having been sold at AGO conventions to folks who used them in the customary way and probably did not even realize those discs also represented an innovative, but ultimately unsuccessful technology.

Some people along the way have asked John or me about Michael's last name, wondering how "no name" in Latin could be someone's actual family name or how a man could get the name of the Captain of the Nautilus. 'Nemo' was Michael's own invention inspired by the pipe organ on the Nautilus. He had endured a very difficult relationship with his father, who was reportedly a severe alcoholic. When Michael had enough age under his belt, he shed his father's name legally and adopted 'Nemo.' Ironically, he then took up with organists many of whom normally drank like fish themselves, while poor Michael sat around being sober.

17 Out on a Limb

Looking back I'm a little surprised that the agency kept making enough money to survive, and to live on to fight another day. Organ recitals were simply not a lucrative business to be in, especially since they were so dependent for sponsorship on support by church groups which viewed them as not at the core of their mission, but decidedly in the category of frills which could easily be sacrificed when the financial going got tough. But, ironically, perhaps it was my church background which helped in this regard. Like most young clergymen of the era I had housing supplied when I was in that business, but in terms of actual money I had to make do with a salary of about $5,000 a year. So, I was not used to a lavish lifestyle any more than were the organists I ended up working with, and for.

I was hardly unique in this budgetary tension, of course. In fact, when I look back I'm actually more surprised that some of my fellow agents for organists survived than I am that my own agency did, because they worked with smaller rosters of, at least in my view, less prominent artists. But they tended to be perhaps more feet-on-the-ground than I was—or to put it another way, many of them may not have been aiming as high as I was. For many of them, it seemed to me, it was more of a hobby than an actual business.

One of them who survived a long time in the business can help to make my point. She was a college teacher throughout her agency work, and a church organist as well, and thus never without steady income from non-agency sources. She also always worked from home, without business rent to worry about, and she kept her roster small enough that she could handle things without a paid assistant—all in all a very sober approach. Of course, the other side of that coin was that she devoted most of her time to non-agency work and thus relegated herself to an avocational status as an agent. (And I do still believe that if one treats any business as small potatoes, one guarantees that it will remain just that.)

I, on the other hand, had leapt in with both feet. That sort of sink-or-swim approach does not square with my assessment of my own personality, and yet the evidence does point in that direction. Virgil Fox had labeled me a "zealot" and maybe he was correct; I may simply not know how to do anything unless I go for broke. And I certainly was not going to attempt being an agent unless it was my true profession and the job had my undivided attention.

From the beginning I believed in buying as much advertising space in the two appropriate professional journals (trade magazines) as it was possible to afford, to the point that my agency grew to be the largest advertiser in TAO for many years, plus a large and steady advertising presence in three other domestic and one foreign trade publication as well.

Then there were the several organizations whose conventions I used as trade shows with their attendant costs for hotel, food, travel, staff salary and expenses, and program booklet advertising (in which we were not infrequently the largest advertiser by far). Several of the smaller organist agencies experimented with this approach as well, for periods of not more than two or so contiguous conventions, but McFarlane never did. They did have a big and consistent presence at national AGO conventions, although they never used the trade show (exhibition booth) approach which so intrigued me.

Then there was office rent with attendant expenses like insurance and commuting costs. To the best of my knowledge every one of the other organist agents had enough sense to run their operations from home and do the work alone, and saved a bundle taking that approach. I'm not really sure of the approach Karen McFarlane took on these scores because, frankly, I just didn't pay enough attention. I know she worked out of office space in her second husband's organ-building company for a time, and I heard once that her successor had an employee, but I really don't know the facts and therefore don't want to draw too much of a comparison with McFarlane about office expenses—except to note that at least most of the other agents for organists didn't have any rent or salaries to pay. Nor did they have our big advertising and promotional costs. Nor were they ever solely dependent on their agency work for a living (except perhaps John McElliott after Karen retired); all had, at least, a church musician's job on the side, as did Karen herself for much, if not all, of her agency career.

So it would seem that I was always reaching for the sky. But failing to keep my feet on the ground may have been, in the long run, the thing that saved PTCA from being just one of the pack of small organists' agencies which came and went during those decades. While always super alert to quality, I also sensed intuitively that quantity had to play an essential role in order for us to thrive in our field. It might have seemed ideal to be able to represent just a small handful of really top-notch performers, but the reality called for more streams of income than that.

Then the needs of the agency clashed in turn with the supply-demand realities of the performance field. Performers (not to mention their agents) had to cope with the frustrations of a market which could not adequately absorb the range of talent available. And eager performers who successfully landed a roster spot with a significant agency had to face a built-in time gap before bookings showed up in any encouraging number. Presenters had to work years (or at least months) ahead in scheduling, so performers new to the scene had to wait their turns for what had to be frustratingly long periods, and many responded by simply giving up and going away. There had to have been far easier ways to make a living. I guess we were all infected with some secret organ bug which we didn't fully understand.

The rhythm of the performance season was also a significant problem if one approached this work on a full-time basis. The organ performance season was strongest in the autumn/early winter and then again in late winter/spring. Because so much of our activity depended on churches (since that's where the instruments were), from Thanksgiving through mid-January was a down period because of Advent/Christmas, and another dry period was waiting in late Lent/Easter-tide. Summer was difficult because a lot of the scene shifted to scattered small series which usually paid only small set honoraria. So, steadiness of income was a big problem and both performers and their agents had to find ways to make approximately half a year of income producing time serve an entire year's worth of expenses—obviously a serious problem for a full-time agency.

Another problem of dealing with organists was that nobody had any money. One of the frequent problems of our early agency era was that the performers often had no way of purchasing their air tickets, and so the agency had to become a banker on top of its other roles, and in many cases to advance the travel money. Of course, the agency didn't have money either. I solved that problem by somehow obtaining a credit card from one of the large U.S. airlines which could be used for these ticket purchases. Then we'd have to wait in fear for the next credit card statement to arrive, and hope that we'd shaved the timing sufficiently for the first fee of the tour to come in before a payment against the ticket had to be made. Usually the timing couldn't be that refined, so the agency had to pay interest charges and then yet again hope something would come in before the *next* statement.

Meanwhile, the presenters themselves may well have gone out on a limb to organize the event and were having trouble rounding up the fee they owed, or had to wait to collect and bank the ticket sales or offering collection before they could write a check for even a portion of the fee which they had agreed to. No one in the entire chain had sufficient money to operate efficiently in those early days, yet we mysteriously managed to keep at it.

This may sound like I'm complaining, but I don't think so; I hope I'm just being descriptive. I don't have much reason to complain in the long run. I did work hard and long in a field which was a bit stingy financially, but I did it voluntarily and successfully.

And, when I finally wanted to retire, the agency lived on. That's a point which carries more weight than it may seem to deserve at a quick glance. There were organists' agencies functioning in this country before either Karen McFarlane or I got into the business. The two most prominent of these were run by women both of whom closed shop during my time, and neither of whom were survived by their agencies despite many years of the agencies' existence. One, as I recall, became ill relatively quickly and at an advanced age and may not have had time to attempt a sale of her business; at any rate no one carried on its work whether she tried to sell or not.

The other of these two agencies fell into the hands of heirs who did try to find someone to carry it forward, and they seemed fairly persistent in that effort. Someone from the heirs contacted me a number of times trying to interest me in buying this agency. I reasoned, however, that the value of the agency was strictly in the artists it represented, and that the agency name had no value to us because our own name was already much stronger and better known.

The several artists involved were not a big temptation either because some of them had been trying to join the PTCA roster in any case, so if I wanted them I did not have to buy an agency to get them. As for the others, I had already applied the hard business measurement that they were not in the same league as most members of the existing PTCA roster, and certainly I did not want to dilute the quality of our roster—and certainly I did not want to pay money to do that in any case. I remember the last of these telephone calls trying to interest me in buying the other agency, and the plaintive resignation of the caller: "So that's it, I guess. Forty years of work on her part and it's not worth anything today."

(A side note in case some reader(s) recognize(s) these agencies from the above comments: There was one substantial artist on the roster of the second agency discussed, so I don't want to accidently give the impression that I thought he was without value. But he had already applied to PTCA more than once in the past and I had felt his talents were too diversified for him to be content with what we might be able to do for him. He's now living in Europe and seems to be fairly successful in a musical performance field which is not tied strictly to the organ.)

Another substantial burden along the way was the cost and enormous hassle of applying for legal visas for our foreign artists to enter the country to perform for income. We did this application process ourselves which saved money but cost dearly in time and effort (and fear of rejection). Karen's agency hired a lawyer to write the applications which saved time and effort but not money. And we both had to endure the necessary revisions and delays which were, at their most mild, excessively frustrating.

The responsible aspect, however, was that we both did go through the legal hoops to protect the performers and our presenters, and to be good corporate citizens. If a performer coming into the country to earn fees were caught without a work visa, the person could be sent home immediately and banned from entering the United States for the foreseeable future.

There were plenty of individual organists whom I have reason to believe entered the country without legal papers, and just gambled that their low profiles would let them avoid detection and thus end up not causing any problem. Occasionally I heard of such a performer (not necessarily always an organist) being caught and sent back on the next plane. A typical reason for detection seemed to be carrying agreement papers or performance contracts with them so that the papers were found by border agents. If the performer claimed to merely be a tourist entering the country on an automatic tourist visa, the performer could usually violate the system with impunity. But if he left performance contracts in plain sight, the best he could claim was ignorance of the law, which didn't impress the border authorities or let them look the other way.

The two longest-lived of the smaller organ agencies during my time avoided the whole problem by having only American performers on their rosters, which saved a lot of headaches and expense (but also limited income, of course). But there were other small agencies showing up and disappearing along the way which did bring over foreign performers. Given the greatly expensive and time-consuming cost of obtaining artist visas, I always harbored suspicions that these agencies just had their performers enter the country as tourists without the proper visas, either not aware of the risk to the performers, or trying to fly under the radar as some kind of church activity.

A detailed account of one difficult visa application can be found in Appendix 4. One of the real problems of the system for the agency was that nothing was guaranteed and all of the work and time investment of setting up a tour could be lost for no income if there were any snags (even just slowness on the part of the Immigration and Naturalization Service) along the way. This had been the case for our entire agency history, but of course after 9/11 it became an even bigger nightmare as the whole system tightened up dramatically.

Another problem we always faced in the visa arena was that INS officials usually had no concept of an organist as a legitimate touring musical performer, and would frequently demand proof of fame and an extensive performance career which many organists could not provide no matter how well known they might be inside the organist community.

These agents interpreted the regulations in light of the big time musical touring groups they knew about from pop culture. So when the names of our performers did not ring a bell for the agent, he assumed, I guess, that someone was trying to use the process for illegitimate purposes. At that point they would demand that we demonstrate that the performer was almost a household name, which for most European organists was, shall we say, a trifle difficult.

So, for organists' agencies which wanted to operate by the book the visa process became another significant disadvantage and expense that freelance performers and less conscientious agencies could avoid (even if it meant technically breaking the law).

Another such expense for PTCA for many years which other agencies blithely escaped was a license to perform fee from the American Society of Composers, Authors and Publishers (ASCAP). Presenting institutions were supposed to either license any particular work not yet in public domain performed on their premises, or to buy a general license for a period of time which would cover anything performed. This included churches, and the larger parishes in big cities or university towns usually did, for the most part, comply I believe. But that left a lot of churches on the sidelines which would be vulnerable to ASCAP harassment if they fell under the spotlight for a public musical event which drew more than routine attention. It was a little more difficult to fly under the radar in presenting a famous European choir to the general public than in staging a concert by one's own church choir (although technically the church choir should have had an ASCAP license itself before performing).

We were touring large English choirs with famous names and reputations, and our presenters were not always the big sophisticated urban churches. It was easy for many of these presenters simply not to be aware of ASCAP requirements, and indeed I was not aware of them either at the beginning of this part of our work. That changed when someone sent one of our tour program booklets to ASCAP in New York (we published a tour program booklet which then went in quantity to each of the presenters for audience distribution, and this may have made it appear that PTCA was the actual presenter rather than the individual venues).

We could have simply written to our presenters reminding them of the licensing requirement, but I instinctively knew that would merely serve as a damper on the willingness of many of our presenters to book our choirs. Most especially it could cut out the smaller presenters for whom one more expense in an already very expensive venture could simply frighten them away. So I decided the agency would instead buy a blanket ASCAP license for each tour, and itself pay the fees which were based on the estimated number of audience members (the system was set up for concert halls which sold tickets and thus had a better handle on such statistics).

McFarlane was the only other "organist agency" which toured choirs in this way, and thus the only other such agency which might have faced the same problem. I never compared notes with them on this topic, however, so I don't know their approach. It's possible they depended on the license each presenting institution or venue was supposed to carry, especially if the ASCAP office never confronted them with the question.

So given the variety of red tape which needed to be complied with to legally tour foreign performers or ensembles, it was perhaps most sensible for the smaller agencies in our field to just avoid the problem by sticking to a roster of only American performers. Some did venture into the more exotic field of foreign performers to a limited extent. I'll probably always suspect they did a lot of cutting of technical corners in doing so, but I'm happy to leave those sorts of concerns far behind at this point—I now hear some of the same tales of frustration about visa applications from Charles that I remember all too well on a first hand basis.

When I approached retirement and tested the waters a bit by putting out word to a few select people that PTCA could become available to a new owner, the reaction was a fair amount of interest in a potential purchase. I think, at the risk of sounding immodest, that PTCA had passed the point that its value was entirely in its roster—the name, history, reputation and culture of the agency now seemed to have its own value, and that in turn seemed to validate my decades in building it. So, I can take it as a point of pride that my agency survived my own time of involvement in its operation and continued to flourish after I left.

None of this on its own changed the existing realities of the organ performance market. I did not rush out to buy a European villa with the proceeds of the agency sale, welcome as those proceeds were. Nor will Charles replace Michael Bloomberg on the list of the nation's richest men by running PTCA henceforth. But the transition proved that I had created and nurtured a legitimate business within a difficult and confined musical field. So, maybe I had demonstrated that it's worth reaching for the stars despite the risk.

The year 2020 has brought unexpected and tremendously difficult challenges, so a future which seemed so promising is now in a limbo of uncertain duration for both PTCA and McFarlane. Most existing bookings have been cancelled or postponed, which leaves both performers and agencies without current income. Even the AGO national convention for this year has been cancelled. I hope both agencies survive and can successfully revive themselves when conditions get better, but it's going to be a heavy lift I suspect.

18. Why Organists are Unique in the Performance Business

(for non-organist readers)

On the road touring organists face a challenge unknown to other musicians. The organist can't carry his instrument around with him like a violinist, although it must be noted that Virgil Fox had already pioneered the concept of moving around a big electronic organ and speakers to otherwise organ-less venues, and that at least one intrepid organist is still trying to make that approach viable today, despite what have to be even greater overhead expenses than in Virgil's day. And the fixed instrument which an organist meets upon arrival at the performance venue can easily be greatly different than the one, or any one, upon which he previously performed.

The touring organist will almost inevitably face an entirely different instrument at each venue. One night it may be a two-manual tracker (mechanical action) organ with "chiffy" Baroque sounds and only a dozen or couple of dozen or so ranks of pipes from which to arrange sound colors, and at the next stop a roaring hundred-plus rank four, or even five manual monster with oceans of romantic/symphonic sounds available.

Control mechanisms will be in different places or missing entirely, similar sounding ranks of pipes will be labeled with different names, the action and response time of the keys and stops will be different, and chances are some well-meaning musician or maintenance man has tried to alter the character of the instrument by nailing open the swell box or re-voicing just the particular ranks a particular performer needed for a particular piece. One performer I know of nearly slid off the other end of the bench on stage when he sat down to play because a helpful maintenance man had polished it to a brilliant perfection.

The same program must be mapped out freshly at each instrument because there are different sounds to work with and because all the controls are bound to be different from the previous instrument performed upon. A professional organ recitalist arranges to have at least an entire day to work with the instrument before the day of the performance, whenever the organist has a choice in the matter, which also increases the overhead cost of travelling to perform. Lots of times that day actually turns out to be a night because the building is open to the public during daylight hours, increasing the difficulty of the task.

Organists & Me

Bad acoustics can plague any performer on the road to some extent, but for the organist the difficulty is compounded because the hall is quite literally the sounding board of the instrument and therefore part of the instrument with an intimacy no other instrumental performer has to cope with. A nice swath of carpet down an aisle can dramatically alter the character of a pipe organ's sound, and almost always for the worse. Ditto for a large winter audience wearing sweaters and coats.

What concert organist has not experienced a sinking awareness that a pedal note was missing as he negotiated the intricacies of a Bach fugue, or had the combination action jam in mid-piece and discovered the maintenance man was outside taking a smoke. And then there is the omnipresent threat of a cypher (a sounding pipe that sticks on even though the organist is no longer pressing the key) at any unexpected time.

The pipe organ is the most complex of musical instruments and there is more to go wrong, and more to be different at the whim of the individual organ builder than any violinist or singer would care even to hear about. And with all of the pedals, keys, and stops to control while performing, the organist has to be more of an athlete than almost any other musician—certainly more than does a pianist at least.

Yet organists seem to be a hearty bunch and usually happy to take the risks in order to experience the unique power of controlling a whole symphony orchestra's worth of sound all by themselves, with only one musical drive and taste in command as the performance unfolds.

19 How to Read an Organist Performer's Bio

It's not easy to build a successful performance career as an organist, yet in each case the agent, or the organist himself must try to make it appear that success has been, or is rapidly being, achieved, especially if the performer is young and just getting started. As you read the promotional bio of an organist, or any other young performer for that matter, it's helpful to A) read between the lines, and B) look for specifics or the lack thereof. (Please note that I'm talking about *performance* bios here, and *not* professional resumes which have an entirely different purpose. The first is to inspire a presenter to book you as a performer, and for the audience at the performance to learn about you as a performer. The second is to use, probably, in trying to find a better job. They may be easy to confuse, but professionalism demands that they not be.)

One of the most frequently used lines you will likely come across is: "has performed extensively in…" or maybe "frequently in…" This line is used to attempt to make a few performances appear to be an established trend. Usually the claim being made will cover the whole country, although sometimes it is reigned in a bit, as in "extensively in New England." The difference is likely between an organist who has performed in a handful of scattered states versus one who has performed only in a handful of states in the same region. In both cases the phrase is used, most likely, to make a very limited performance history sound impressive. (I don't say this because I lack sympathy for the uphill battle needed to surface as a performer; trying to help organists achieve that transition, after all, was my life's work.)

If a performer has really performed "extensively" you are likely to see more specificity, perhaps by giving the number of states, or countries, or continents which actually apply. I know the problem faced by the agents and performers well, and I've been forced to rely on this phrase myself many times—actually, it almost feels like I invented it. The problem, in essence, forces one to take a genuine, but unimpressive, number of professional performances and make them seem impressive, i.e. to take a relatively unknown performer and make him sound as if he is widely known, admired, and busy performing professionally—to sound like much more than merely a local phenomenon.

Just to refer to this country alone, only one of my performers managed to perform in every U.S. state during my tenure: Paul Jacobs. Several others came close. One of those, Christopher Houlihan, was so close to that mark at the agency transition that I have no doubt he will achieve it soon. For many very good performers, however, that goal is appealing but elusive. And part of the problem for organists specifically is that large areas of the country host very few fee-paying recitals. A really professional artist's bio will give specifics rather than gloss claims, at least until the point that the performer's name is so well known that it stands as its own credential.

The dubious point about claiming lots of European performing experience is that so many of these events are part of summer series which pay no, or very small honoraria, and thus apply fairly casual criteria to selecting performers from among the many who clamor to fill the slots. As in the U.S., series which have a lot of events each season draw a lot of performers happy to accept a small set honorarium. If a bio claims a lot of performances at St. Thomas Fifth Avenue, or St. Patrick's Cathedral, or Trinity Wall Street and other venues which feature lots of organists and offer set fees, if any, you can safely read it as an indication that the performer is not, or is not yet, drawing many standard professional fee-paying bookings (and that anything in New York City sounds pretty "big time" successful back home in Grand Forks).

Again, this is not to say that some of these performers lack talent, but only that they are trying to convey the sense of career success by way of slim credentials (or maybe I should say they are almost forced to try to convey that sense in this way).

Another deception (intentional or not) used by some agents and performers is to quote praise without attribution of the quotation. If the performer has a genuine newspaper or journal quotation to use, he will not use superlatives in quotation marks in his bio without saying who said or wrote the praise. "Excellent organist" is nice, but it means something only if it came from a source beyond the performer's mother or uncle. I was constantly frustrated during my working life at PTCA by agents and artists who used unattributed quotations—it was possible someone might have actually used the superlative to describe the organist's work, but who? To let the praising phrase hang out in mid-air without attribution was clearly an attempt to suggest that it represented a consensus of audience reactions.

Was it the organist's roommate, or *The Wall Street Journal*? Since no attribution was made, it obviously was not the *WSJ*, and probably was, in fact, just a friend or relative of the performer. This put at a disadvantage the honest performers who had actually earned critical praise from legitimate professional sources. Hopefully this approach is not as prevalent today; at least the worst offending organists' agent from my day is no longer on the scene. Yet even today I still see paid advertisements in TAO which contain nothing but a list of unattributed phrases of praise; phrases which have quotation marks around them but are presented as if they arose spontaneously out of the vapor. In using this approach, the artist actually makes himself vulnerable to the suspicion that no one at all said the quoted phrase; that the agent or artist simply made it up.

As a veteran of the very difficult business of getting professional critical attention for my artists, I can assure you that if good reviews are alluded to or quoted without attribution, they simply don't exist. If *The New York Times* (for example) says anything remotely quotable about a performer, that quotation will be used and credited, and Aunt Susan's comments will no longer be needed. Please note I'm not accusing performers of dishonesty *per se* when they use unattributed praise; probably somebody along the way did say this or that. Maybe it was a student of the performer. But if it is left unattributed it was because the performer realized that the speaker's identity would not contribute any weight, so leaving off the source of the quotation may not have been technically dishonest, but it was certainly somewhat intentionally deceptive.

I always suspected this tendency to use unattributed quotations was somehow connected with the link between organ performance and church music—the church context somehow failed to hold performers to a rigid standard of professionalism. In church, all would be forgiven even when it fell short of rigid accuracy or specificity, so both performers and agents could be lulled into a sense of not really needing to adhere to truly professional standards. That seemed to make difficult-to-attain critical quotations available to more performers because no one in the church context would challenge just who had actually said "a fine performance;" a newspaper, or a fan? Out in the real world of secular musical performers quite a bit more discipline had to be observed.

Charles Miller, my successor, has also reminded me that one of the major difficulties organists have in getting reviewed by major critics is that they often have institutional policies (or personal prejudices) against reviewing events held in a church—and of course most performance-worthy organs are, indeed, in churches. "When I was in Washington DC I don't know how many times I begged and pleaded with the *Washington Post* critic Anne Midgette to review a major organist or choral event at National City Christian Church," he said. "She would not set foot in the place!"

In writing this I looked up the current bios on the websites of just two American-based organists, both without agents, both of whom label themselves as "international" performers, and I found these three over-reaching descriptions of themselves without any supporting evidence offered: "Acclaimed," "Renowned worldwide," and "frequently appears." These two organists also awarded themselves self-critical phrases such as "Stunningly inspirational" and "Rigorous private studies."

Organists & Me

Here's a line from one such performer's bio: "Critically acclaimed as a 'world class talent,' John Doe is in frequent demand...." Dear Mr. Doe, if you want us to believe you may actually be such a talent based on these words, please give us at least one example of who says you are. And if you want to be fair to your fellow organist performers who work very hard to earn legitimate critical testimonials, please don't claim to have some unless you are willing to let us know where they came from.

Such exercises in creative writing may owe something to the church context in which most organists operate. Church is a context in which one is unlikely to be challenged on any claim because no one wants to make anyone else unhappy or to rile the waters, and most church members know so little about the organ performance scene that almost any claim seems possible to them. The same organist working in an academic setting would probably need to be more circumspect in describing his standing and credentials.

Another odd view of legitimacy often turned up in organists' bios during my time: press bios which began with an agency credit rather than ending with one, which was the industry standard if the agency was mentioned at all in the bio text. This approach was constantly used by a one-woman agency which started many of its artist bios with "Dr. Jones is represented by Jane Doe Organists Management." This always seemed to me to be a blazing neon sign that the performer had very little going for him, if indeed his biggest career accomplishment was merely being on the roster of a tiny one-agent-one-instrument-only agency. Was this approach just a manifestation of the agent's runaway ego? Perhaps that was indeed part of the picture, but I think the real problem the writer of the bio faced was the lack of anything more impressive to say.

This approach also highlighted the strange assumption by so many organists that merely having an agent was a big career accomplishment—a major credential in and of itself, and a sign that one was pulled out of the ranks of merely good church organists and dropped into the rarified ranks of "concert" organists. It was also an indication of how isolated from the mainstream concert stage most organists were as performers.

As usual with organists, many of them seemed to equate church music, and specifically working as a choirmaster, with performance as a professional organist performer in their stage bios. A current one (and a somewhat typical one) on the web states, "She has over fifteen years of experience in church music, having led volunteer and professional choir programs...." How is this a credential for being a soloist with a symphony orchestra or a recitalist at, say, Alice Tully Hall on Broadway? And why should it be of interest to an audience in either case? Another current web bio takes this confusion a step further by extolling the organist's work as an

How to Read an Organist Performer's Bio

"accompanist" in a variety of places, while evidently assuming this adds to his credentials as a "concert" level performer—two very different things it would seem to me.

Organists often enough seemed to headline their performance bios with their church position, making it the very first sentence audience members at a performance would read. It seemed, and still seems, to me that this introduces an unnecessary apples-and-oranges tension into the story. Yes, the performer had a day job in order to stay afloat financially, which is perfectly legitimate. But when was the last time you saw an actor's bio in a theater program which began: "John Doe waits tables at a local restaurant when he is not on stage…."? (Yes, I know being a church organist is not the equivalent of waiting tables and, yes, I know some will be quick to take offense. But from the perspective of professional performance, I think the analogy is legitimate.)

My frustration with the way organists often presented themselves in their performance bios many times focused on violations of the most rudimentary rules of good journalism, such as adding their own descriptive adjectives. It was certainly okay to write that a specific journal called the organist's playing of this or that "electrifying," but something else entirely to add descriptive adjectives oneself: "he is known for his electrifying performance of this or that school of music…"

Then there was the frequent violation of the tried and true merit of leading with the most salient and consequential aspects of the story and working down to more mundane information. I've lost count of the organist bios I've seen which began, "John Doe was born in Podunck." This slavish adherence to chronology and lack of prioritizing information surely stopped many a reader in his tracks before reaching the more relevant material. (Some human interest material can be a good thing to include in an artist's bio, but only after the direct and germane musical material has been covered.)

One of my goals during my agency years was to nudge the organ scene a little further along in its commitment to professionalism in terms of self-expression and written materials; the extent to which I may have helped in that regard is unknowable.

As was frequently the case, there I was with my fixation on the organ as a stand-alone concert or soloist instrument, not dependent on the church for legitimacy or identity. Surely there were others who had the same concerns, but my position always felt a bit lonely. The organists, as a tribe however, seemed perfectly happy to keep the focus mostly on church music even when they were performing before a non-church audience. I'd like to think I helped move the needle a little bit, but if so I don't believe it was very far. The young organists of today will have to keep pushing in that direction themselves for progress to be made, and for some reason I feel reasonably optimistic about them doing so.

20 Glancing Back

I've had the pleasure of working with a wide variety of gifted musicians along the way, who have exhibited a wide variety of tastes and personality. This list hardly exhausts their colorful antics, but I hope it will give you some sense of our colorful ranks. Many of these vignettes offer personal rather than arms-length memories, but I think approaching these artists as people, as well as performers, is a legitimate and more interesting approach. Needless to say they were all outstanding musicians and performers, and I trust readers to appreciate that, even though I may not spell it out at each entry or be able to include each performer we worked with.

PAUL BISACCIA (AMERICAN PIANIST):

Aside from his enormous musical talent, Paul is one of the most industrious and optimistic people I've ever known. These three qualities taken together made for a sure-fire attractive personality and magnetic stage presence. Paul was never afraid to work very hard on any facet of his career, and never wasted time worrying about his chances of success in advance—he just plowed ahead, leaving many less industrious peers in the dust. The result of this driven optimism also made Paul one of the most gratifying artists I had the pleasure of working with. If he ever felt I'd under performed for him (which he never indicated had crossed his mind) he would not have wasted his own time or energy complaining. Not Paul; he would have gathered his wits and launched another inventive campaign to advance his performance career. Paul also had a sure-fire grasp of how to entertain while performing serious music, an instinct which let him race past some of his peers who merely had technique and talent.

RAGNAR BJÖRNSSON (ICELAND):

Walking together in New York while discussing business, I was thrown off guard when we started to cross Fifth Avenue and he grabbed my left arm and looped his arm through mine as if we were on a date. Evidently it's an Icelandic custom even for men when walking together. Working with our foreign artists was always a cultural education.

BOSTON BRASS (QUINTET):

Agency hopping was not unknown in organist circles, but it was fairly endemic in the wider musical performance scene. Boston Brass had approached us seeking representation, and we had launched a relationship which was yielding some success in bookings even in the very early stages. The ensemble had expressed no particular frustrations to me, but evidently was still trying to 'better' itself because I was informed a few months into our relationship that it had been accepted by a small New York agency and wanted to cancel our contract. I think the "New York" address of the other agency was perhaps its biggest attraction because I can't even remember the agency's name at this point; it was not a major player in any case.

With less than a year of our work on the quintet's behalf, and with bookings in place but always requiring a long lead time, I decided not to roll over and play dead (which required some strength of character for a church boy of my background). So I advised them they would have to buy out their contract with PTCA rather than my just waving good-bye. One of them then had to drive to Hartford from Boston with a check and work out the details with my partner Ray. This was the only time in my long agency career in which I stood on a contract technicality with an artist-client. A few years later there was a similar situation with the Rastrelli Cello Quartet, which had also approached us seeking representation, although they wanted to move on only about two or three months into our relationship; again, the 'gain' for them was getting an agent with a New York address. This time, although annoyed, I didn't care enough to do anything *except* wave good-bye. The music business was surprisingly fickle and cutthroat, but one of the fringe benefits of working mostly with organists was that, being so tied to the church, they were generally well intentioned and did give some thought to the agent's situation as well as their own.

RAYMOND & ELIZABETH CHENAULT (USA, GEORGIA):

This husband-wife team pioneered the duo-organist performance approach and then generously endowed the art form with many compositions for organ-four-hands-four-feet which they commissioned from their own resources (over 70 of them by now). Their performances, at least in my day, usually concluded with a stirring rendition of John Philip Sousa's "Stars and Stripes Forever" which they had transcribed for organ themselves. Their example gave rise to several other duo-organist teams along the way, but it was "The Chenaults" which became synonymous with the concept of two organists performing from one bench.

JAMES DAVID CHRISTIE (USA, MASSACHUSETTS):

During my period on the organ scene one of its most obvious characteristics was a tension between a faction which favored older (pre-Bach and maybe Bach) literature, tracker organs, and certain historical fingerings, etc., let's call them 'traditionalists' for lack of a better word, and another faction which favored newer literature (Bach and later), could accept electro-pneumatic instruments, etc. The 'traditionalists' always carried an air of righteousness about them, feeling they were the authentic organists and that the others were somehow almost the heretics of the organ world. The other camp sometimes referred to these ultra-traditionalists as not just the pre-Bach organists, but as the "pre-music" crowd.

I think these distinctions are gradually fading quite a bit in the 21st century, but for most of the late 20th century and into this one they were a prominent, and fairly rigid, aspect of the scene. Jim Christie (he was always careful to remind me that his name technically was James David as though hyphenated) was the chief member of our roster representing the 'traditionalists.' And he was superb at it, probably the finest and most communicative American performer of this early organ literature. By virtue of our respective personalities he and I were never close friends in the usual sense of the word, but we were both professionals who got along and worked together easily. While my own musical tastes frequently ran in the Bach and post-Bach direction, my admiration for Jim Christie was genuine and very respectful.

PETER RICHARD CONTE (USA, PENNSYLVANIA):

Peter certainly held the most unusual organist post of any PTCA roster member, presiding as he did at a very large symphonic style instrument in a center-city Philadelphia department store (now Macy's, previously Lord & Taylor, originally Wannamaker's). While the department store instrument was decidedly not a church organ, he was also a church organist in addition, holding the loft at a very 'high church' Episcopal parish in the city.

The department store job gave him free reign to program transcriptions, which would have to have been considered daring for the time in most other contexts. Peter had a natural talent and instinct for transcriptions, and arranged many himself. He also had the courage to use them in the church position too, and I used to hear grousing from 'purist' sources about preludes which were sometimes transcriptions of opera arias. So Peter early-on was regarded by some as one of the organ world's sinners, although as time went on and tastes changed in the direction of transcriptions, he became one of the scene's saints. He was also, to my memory, a great improvisator but that carried no negative freight because organists had decided long ago that the great French organist improvisators were to be admired.

NICHOLAS DANBY (ENGLAND):
His name reminds me of the foibles of human memory (mine at least) because when I see it I always think of the small German restaurant he discovered in Hartford and enjoyed on his several performance trips here. Intellectually I know I enjoyed his performance work many times, and that his personality was interesting far beyond his food preferences, but my mind always goes back to the little restaurant (at which I never ate, and which is no longer with us) and refuses to yield more information.

LYNNE DAVIS (USA, MICHIGAN):
I always thought of Lynne as somehow suspended between two worlds: the unpretentious girl from Michigan who got caught up in the whirl of fashion, music, education and even politics in Paris but perhaps never completed the transition, at least in so far as making France her permanent home. Her husband was the scion of a well-known French family which included the inventor of a popular printing type-face, and I believe her daughter understandably considers herself French rather than American. But Lynne, while savoring the French connection and proud to use it to shape her career when opportunity presented itself, remained to some measure the American girl from East Lansing. She seemed at times to see no reason she could not be both that Midwestern girl and the French sophisticate at the same time. More than once she reacted to a list of artists invited to perform at an AGO convention to be held in Michigan by asking me, "Why didn't they invite me? I'm from East Lansing." After she became a relatively young widow she did return to the United States for a university teaching position, at which she continues to embrace a certain French pedigree to complete her personal and professional profile.

One of her memorable innovations as a performer was to link up with some of the leading Parisian couture houses and model one or more (sometimes several) dress creations while on stage as an organist. This unique performance idea started when she was to perform at the United States Embassy in Paris and borrowed a dress from the famed French designer Hubert de Givenchy to lend some particularly French glamor to the occasion.

There's a little bit of Lynne painted on me with some regularity even in my retirement. Quite a few years ago in Chartres, after giving us a tour of the stained glass museum her husband had contributed to the city, she wanted to load everyone into her car to drive us to the chateau she and her husband were living in at the time. I was there with John and Ray. Lynne's mother was visiting France at the time as well. We were all in Lynne's car ready to roll except for Mama who was happily chatting with someone while the engine idled. Finally Lynne's patience gave out. She opened the driver's window and spoke with an iron mixture of icy authority and totally spent patience: "Mother, get in the car!" I've managed to grow older now by some unforeseen circumstance, and sometimes dither a bit getting ready to be driven somewhere, or take way too long physically contorting myself into the passenger seat. Suddenly there is sure to be a souvenir of Lynne Davis. Ray, a capable mimic of anyone he's ever met, is almost sure to deliver another: "Mother, get in the car!"

ISABELLE DEMERS (CANADA, QUEBEC):
A real French Canadian from Montreal. I can't help wondering how she adjusted to life in Waco, Texas, of all places, but she bought her own house there, so Baylor University must agree with her to some significant extent. Please don't tell on me for questioning life in Waco however; I'm sure it has its good points (see Driskill-Smith below). From the time she joined the PTCA roster, Isabelle was one of our most booked artists, and Charles Miller tells me that's still the case. Isabelle was, and I'm sure still is, noted and loved for her sharp sense of humor, often very dryly delivered.

ANDREW DEWAR (ENGLAND):
In a charming way Andrew illustrated the likelihood that heterosexuals probably felt a little out of their element inside the community of organists, especially in this country. At a post-recital private reception (attended only by gays) the prevailing curiosity got the better of someone who, after a few drinks, asked him whether or not he was gay. "No, but my brother is," Andy responded without the slightest pause between the "no" and the "but." It was as though he could not quite meet the expectation himself, but was happy and ready to use his brother as the missing credential.

CLIVE DRISKILL-SMITH (ENGLAND):
Clive is as proper an Englishman as you'd want to encounter, although never stuffy. I remember the careful delicacy and tact with which he let me know, with exquisite subtlety, that he would be grateful for an invitation to use our Florida house for a few days during a gap in one of his American tours. And memorable, too, was his gentlemanly gesture of thanks for the favor.

I knew he felt the usual financial pinch English ecclesiastical organists learn to accept as their plight, and I knew his idea of a solution was to find a job in the United States (an idea that had occurred to quite a few British organists). I was surprised, however, after my retirement from the agency, when he accepted an opportunity to exchange the rarified civilization of Oxford and Christ Church for the occasional frontier rough edges of Texas.

I'm sure Clive has the personality resources to flourish there, but please don't tell the Fort-Worth Chamber of Commerce what I just said—I'm not the one who first observed that the American East stops in Dallas and the American West begins in Fort Worth.

ETON COLLEGE CHOIR (ENGLAND):
Some of my most joyful and educational experiences as an agent came from working with several of the legendary English choirs of men and boys. Their level of musical quality and performance achievement were stunning to behold, but they also gave me a window of insight into the English "public schools" tradition and thus into that key segment of the English character. On one return visit to Eton after the choir had completed a successful American tour, I followed the choir out of Evensong down one of the winding turret stairways of the chapel.

One of the older boys turned to me and thanked me by name for giving them the opportunity to tour abroad. I didn't know his name and had had no individual contact with him, and so was all the more struck by his poise, graciousness, eloquence, and self-assurance in volunteering engagement with a visiting American. In a sudden flash, as it were, I could begin to understand the weight these elite schools had in forming and maturing the English character and the great English leaders.

Another time under similar circumstances at Christ Church, Oxford, I was struck when one of the younger boys in procession recognized me with a startled facial expression but didn't miss a step in keeping to the discipline of the choir routine. This time we did know each other as individuals, and had been nearly friends for a couple days. When I noticed him sitting alone on a choir tour bus in Iowa while all the other boys were sitting in pairs, I sat next to him and we started the easy conversation which these bright kids could hold so easily with adults. Just in casual conversation he left traces of his astonishing knowledge of history and culture. I was very pleased to see him again in Oxford, although our exchange had to be non-verbal in the circumstance. I wondered what an American kid of his age would have done—would he have broken ranks with the procession, or waved heartily at the expense of the formality expected of him? These English public school (prep-school) boys were an intriguing peek behind the curtain into a culture which may have spawned America, but from which America had so dramatically moved on. As much as I enjoyed England as a tourist, these associations with the choirs of her elite institutions provided insights which would never have been available to me as a standard-issue tourist.

JEAN-LOUIS GIL (FRANCE):
He is a figure who to me remains always young and always tragic in the same way as many Americans remember John F. Kennedy. He and his

boyfriend, Jean-Noel, were John's age and became our friends beyond the business relationship, whether played out in France or the U.S. Jean-Noel sometimes stayed with us while Jean-Louis was off touring in another part of the country. Then one day came the incomprehensible news that Jean-Noel had taken his own life in Paris. I recall only that HIV/AIDS, the great scourge of gay life in the late 20th century, was involved. Later came more news, this time that Jean-Louis had married his school-boy girlfriend. She came along with him on his last performance tour in the U.S. and visited us in South Orange (Newark) as had Jean-Noel. But Jean-Louis could not outrun the plague even with a wife, and he became, to the best of my knowledge, only the second or third member of our long-running roster of artists to die from the complications of HIV/AIDS, although not the only one to die young and still in his touring years as a performer.

STEWART WAYNE FOSTER (USA, FLORIDA):

He was the first winner of the Dallas International Organ Competition and to the best of my memory one of the earliest (maybe the first from an ongoing regular competition) performers on our roster by virtue of a competition win. We became personal friends when he got a church job in Charleston SC and set up shop there. John and I had a house in Charleston at the time, and so we were neighbors for parts of the year. Wayne, as he was known by one and all, was the kind of guy anyone was happy to have around, but also the kind of guy not likely to do or say anything with enough edge to turn it into an anecdote. Much later, despite a fairly successful booking rate, he became the first, and I think only, of our roster members to simply decide he didn't enjoy performing enough for the hassle involved, and informed me he just wanted to drop out of the recital scene. That left him in his native Florida at a church job with minimal pressure, and contented, I hope. I'm told that Wayne is indeed happy now, which puts me in the strange position of being grateful that one of our most talented artists gave up on the whole idea of being a performer.

ROBERT GLASGOW (USA, OKLAHOMA):

He was one of America's greatest proponents of and teachers of the symphonic organ school during the 20th century. During his long tenure at the University of Michigan he also found an unusual way to relate to students beyond the classroom. He liked to travel but evidently not to do all the driving, and so he constantly invited students to go on trips with him and share the driving. I'm told by Charles Miller that these trips also involved stops along the way to hear noteworthy instruments or even for coaching sessions with notable organ teachers. Glasgow evidently paid for the meals on such trips, and Charles tells me he often treated the last student of the day at Michigan to a meal as well.

In this way, unintentionally, he gave Ray his first serious boyfriend and our agency a several year staff member of special and consequential importance. Charles had driven Glasgow to the Connecticut shore where Glasgow liked to stay with Ron Stalford, Music Director at All Saints' Church in Worcester, at Ron's summer home. John and Ray had been on the road for business and stopped into the same enclave of shoreline homes to visit Chester Cooke and the Yale organist Thomas Murray. They came across the Glasgow crew on the next door porch and Ray returned home with a story about the cute university kid he'd met, but the subject was dropped until a series of notes from Michigan began arriving by post. Enough to say that in due course Charles was living with us in Hartford and serving, for almost a decade, as booking director of Phillip Truckenbrod Concert Artists. After a few further decades of circumnavigation Charles has found his way back to Michigan where he has headquartered PTCA which he now owns.

CHRISTOPHER HERRICK (ENGLAND):

I managed to get this English organist a rather splendid (and decently paid) showcase at Lincoln Center in New York in which he performed the complete organ works of J.S. Bach in a series of festival recitals at Alice Tully Hall. Illustrative of the attitude so many artists seemed to have about their agents, viewing them more as necessary evils than partners, Herrick never quite accepted that I was the reason he got the gig. Even after the series concluded he asked again, "You mean they didn't ask for me specifically to be the performer?" No, Christopher, in fact they started out wanting someone from a different agency roster altogether.

MICHAEL HEY (NEW YORK):

Michael is one of those genuinely nice guys one is privileged to meet from time to time, and he was also one of the straight organists on our roster—a fact I had to learn to my embarrassment.

At the last Washington DC AGO national convention of my active career, John's and my hotel room had become something of a gathering place for wind down and a little wine at day's end. We had a young organist friend who usually stopped by who, although we'd known him for some time, was a mystery to us as to his sexuality. So we played it safe by avoiding any compromising discussion which might cause him uneasiness. That necessity was not uncommon. Once our friend Robert Edward Smith was driving a bunch of Trinity College students in his van after a chapel service. Riding next to him was the intern assistant chaplain, and after Robert stopped to let the students out, he turned to this guy with relief and said, "Good. Now we can talk gay." "Oh, no we can't," came the reply, as the intern pointed back to one straggler student sprawled in the back of

Robert's van. "Now we can talk gay" had thus become one of our private little jokes; a bit of group shtick.

Anyway, in our Washington hotel room our young friend joined us one convention evening together with Christopher Houlihan who was rooming at the convention with his friend from Juilliard, Michael Hey. Houli and Michael had stretched out on our beds because the rest of us occupied the only chairs in the room, and we all chatted away happily. The young guy of undetermined sexuality decided it was time to sleep and left the room to retire. "Good. Now we can talk gay," I blurted out, thinking I was being cute. "Oh, no we can't," Houli repeated from memory, pointing to Michael. I was abashed, but Michael, as always, was so graceful, sweet and accepting that before long we were indeed talking gay again, and with him enjoying it as much as the three gay guys.

Michael now performs not only as a recitalist, but in duo with his wife who is a recognized violinist. And he holds one of the country's most prominent organist posts as Associate Director of Music and Organist at St. Patrick's Cathedral on Fifth Avenue, New York.

CHRISTOPHER HOULIHAN (USA, CONNECTICUT):
I've always tried to avoid comparing artists we represented even though I must have been asked hundreds of times which one I thought was the biggest talent, so I don't want to start now—besides, I don't really believe performers can be realistically compared; the factors involved being so peculiar to the particular listener.

I can, however, say which artist gave me the most satisfaction and sense of accomplishment to work with. "Houli" was always responsive to anything that I suggested might help in his career building efforts and was grateful as well as cooperative. He truly accepted the agent as a valuable ally and partner, as many performers seemed to find difficult to do. That made working with him a pleasure, and it helped speed his career advancement along at an impressive clip. If I sometimes wonder what I actually accomplished with my half-century commitment to the cause of organs and organists, I do not doubt that I helped give the musical world a worthy performer of constantly growing potential in Christopher, and that this contribution will benefit the cause of the organ as a legitimate concert instrument well into the future.

Houli spent a year studying in France, not all that unusual for an American organist, but during that time he was appointed assistant cathedral musician at the American Cathedral in Paris, and it was unusual for an American student to hold any such position. He also had the distinction there of playing for a visiting American president (George W. Bush) on a Sunday when the titular organist was away and he had inherited the whole musical responsibility, including conducting the choirs.

Organists & Me
DAVID HURD (USA, NEW YORK):
David was the first performer to join our roster as a result of winning a competition, this one being that of the International Congress of Organists held in Philadelphia (1977). That was lucky for the agency as much as it may have been for the performer. And to boot, he is a great guy whose easy personality was always a bonus.

What David taught me most specifically, however, was not musical but psychological. After he performed at Trinity College during our first year living in Hartford, we invited him and his friends who had come up from New York City for the recital over to our new apartment for an after-glow. This town-house style apartment had a guest bathroom next to the kitchen on the lower level which we cleaned carefully for the event. It also had a bathroom off each bedroom on the main floor, and we figured there was no real need to clean them up especially since we had prepared the guest toilet. At the gathering when the first person asked to use the restroom we naturally directed them to the lower floor. There was a strange hesitation and we could sense that something had not been well received. I then said, okay, there are two bathrooms on this floor as well, but beware that we had not especially cleaned them for the evening. I don't remember how it was all resolved, but after our guests left John and I figured out the problem. We must have seemed to these black guys to be protecting our own bathrooms from them by sending them to the lower floor. It was a quick and unexpected lesson to a couple of white guys in how black Americans have learned from sad experience to be alert for signs of discrimination. This felt really upsetting, and we kicked ourselves for not being able to predict their reaction—of course, it was not our fault either that the designer of the place had decided to locate the guest bathroom on the bottom floor, below the main living area.

The lesson was repeated and expanded during the years we represented the New England Spiritual Ensemble. I learned a lot about personal grace from those friendly singers, and also how to worry like a parent; especially when they would take off from Boston in a couple of cars headed into the deep south on performance tour. "Driving while black" became a vivid cause for concern for me even though I was sitting in an office in New England. One never really knows what it's like to 'walk in someone else's shoes' but these performers helped me fit into the human race with a little more honesty than I might have achieved without them.

David was widely recognized and honored as a composer and as a major influence in the musical life of the Episcopal Church. In fact, he collected honorary doctorates like some folks collect antiques. During one short period no fewer than three theological seminaries honored him with degrees: Church Divinity School of the Pacific in California, Seabury-

Western Theological Seminary in Illinois, and Berkeley Divinity School at Yale University.

PAUL JACOBS (USA, PENNSYLVANIA):

Paul is one of the very top American concert organists and therefore his inclusion in this selection of vignettes is nearly required. But he is, for me, also the most difficult to write about of the many people I've represented. This is probably true largely because our professional relationship almost immediately turned into a close friendship, which then over the years diminished somehow into a cool and pragmatic strictly-business series of transactions. It would probably seem logical that such an evolution in a relationship had two equal actors, but the difficulty is that I don't see it, nor did I ever feel it, in that way. To me, it doesn't feel that I'm the one who changed. However, I may indeed be the one responsible for the change, at least partially.

When Paul, right after getting his Yale master's degree, was offered the replacement spot for his own teacher, John Weaver, on the organ faculty at the Juilliard School in New York, he instead wanted to return to a church job he had felt very comfortable with in suburban Philadelphia. I urged him to stay in New York, confident that he would flourish in that more varied, more challenging, and much more visible setting. I think history proved me right, but as Paul soared he also had less time for anything but an aggressive pursuit of his own image of himself. Nevertheless, I consider it one of my significant contributions to the organ performance field to have helped Paul achieve the elevated status he enjoys, and has earned, today. And, for that matter, I'm hardly the only agent whose contributions to a performer may have been under-appreciated; it's almost part of the job description.

Paul did have a large impact on the quality of organ performance in this country, and for that it would be wrong to fail to credit and thank him. In very large measure, among other things, he is responsible for so many of our concert artists performing from memory now, and thus standing their ground on stage with pianists. And it should be noted that pianists have a far easier job playing from memory than do organists, with the organists' need to maneuver several keyboards at once plus a pedalboard, and the need to change registrations along the course of a piece of music. Paul was my great ally in trying to spotlight the pipe organ as a musical instrument legitimate in its own right, and not merely as an adjunct to church worship.

It should be noted, too, that Paul won a Grammy Award, the first and so far only solo organist ever to have done so. Yes, I was enormously proud of Paul Jacobs, and at least for a time, he appeared to be of me as well.

I recently discovered a file of letters from Paul I'd saved from his days just before and during his master's degree program at Yale. They are a charming throw back to a more innocent period, all hand written and all full of wonder at the world as it unfolded for him and excitement at his developing career, and all signed "Your Friend." After he set up shop in New Haven it was also rather charmingly old-fashioned to be exchanging notes on paper across a gulf of just forty miles or so. These letters speak plaintively of his struggles to adapt to Yale and of his temptation to transfer to Juilliard where, ironically, he would himself eventually lead one of the strongest organ study programs in the country.

NICOLAS KYNASTON (ENGLAND):

Nicolas was as close to being my brother as any friend I've met along the organist highway. We were almost exactly the same age and both of our personalities had been heavily shaped by a staunchly religious upbringing, he a Roman Catholic and me a Lutheran (which in a lot of surprising ways are not all that different). Nicolas was, I think, the most candid and open in his conversations with me of any of the artists I represented during my half century of work in the field. There was one major point of distinction, however. Nicolas was genuinely heterosexual. I was not.

By some weird chemistry that difference did not inhibit our closeness; I think it actually strengthened it. He was a very open personality, and socially fearless. How it began I can't recall, but we fell into the habit of socializing and eating at gay clubs in London. Freddie Symonds, my English friend and for a time business partner, knew the scene well and had initiated John and me into some of its bright spots. Nicolas was always game, and happy actually, to go along for the ride. Although a deeply religious Catholic (and former Organist of London's Westminster Cathedral), there was not a shred of judgement or repudiation on his part, and he always seemed healthily curious to learn how the other half lived.

Our last communication, after we both had begun to close down our careers with the organ, told of the untimely death of his young adult son Gabriel in Paris. Nicolas was obviously devastated, and I knew how much he loved the young man and identified him as the future. I was again left to contemplate one of the recurring themes of my own life, that the loss of someone close out of the normal sequence of age means that part of one's own future has died. I tried my best to write a letter which was sympathetic, but the right words to use in such a situation do not come easily to any mortal.

DOUGLAS LAWRENCE (AUSTRALIA):

When he stayed with us a few nights in Newark while on tour here, we took him to dinner at a local restaurant which (unfortunately) offered live entertainment. With impeccable timing, we had accidently picked an evening when the show was a singer with back-up instrumentalists doing a program of Australian folk music. Mid-meal suddenly Douglas had left the table, and there he was standing in front of the singer, arms akimbo, and staring into his face from a handful of inches away. The poor guy managed to keep going a couple of minutes more before he had to switch off his microphone and find out why some nutcase was starring him down in the middle of a performance.

After a few minutes of amplification silence but arms flying and wild gesticulations between the two, Douglas returned to our table and the music started again. It turned out that there was something about the performance of "Waltzing Matilda" which the Australian found insulting and had to protest in his typically robust manner. "It was bloody wrong," was the verdict he brought back to our table. That didn't tell us very much, but we did not seek details, being just grateful for a public truce.

JEAN-PIERRE LEGUAY (FRANCE):
Following in the footsteps of Louis Vierne Jean-Pierre was titular organist (actually one of three at the same time) of Notre Dame Cathedral in Paris, a composer for the organ—and, also like Vierne, he was blind. He was a graduate of the French school for the blind which had taught Vierne and had contributed other French blind organists of note. Once at the console he could fly on his own and soar with the eagles. But robbed of his home perch he had to depend on others, and needed someone to accompany him when he toured, which unfortunately cut his performance fees in half effectively. Usually his wife was able to make the trip over, but at times that duty fell to her sister.

GEORGE MCPHEE (SCOTLAND):
George was (since 1963 and still is at the time of this writing) the organist of Paisley Abbey, one of the many ancient British structures repurposed from Catholic to Protestant control after the Reformation. And he was certainly one of Scotland's leading organists. One quick memory was his story about British central heating; how ice would form overnight on his bathroom wash basin at home. He also inadvertently provided me a lesson in never trusting a commercial printer without proofing the copy first (this was in a by-gone era of printing). I had ordered a few thousand flyers for use in promoting him, and when they were delivered I found myself staring at a big, bold "George McPee" on the obverse side.

MICHAEL MURRAY (USA, OHIO):
For a time Michael had the best recording career going of any American organist at the time, with a home-town label of national distribution, Telarc, issuing one release after another and keeping him as its sole organist. Despite that advantage we found it difficult to work together in the long run. I was receiving concerned reviews from various audience members and

presenters about his live performances (not his recorded ones), and decided to share one of them that seemed fairly level-headed, thinking it might help Michael to know how some people were reacting. He wrote back, "I do not thank you for sending that note," and dropped off the agency roster in apparent response.

We had also been close as a couple with Michael and his partner Gary. The relationship started very pleasantly and we even scheduled a holiday together by renting a lake-side cottage in New Hampshire one summer. When we pulled up to the site (Michael and Gary had arrived first) complete with our dog, Gary came running out to advise us, "Don't even get out of your car." Michael was dissatisfied with the cleanliness of the cabin and had already booked us for the night at the university hotel at Dartmouth in nearby Hanover. Somehow we managed to sneak the dog into our room without incident. The next time we scheduled a trip together in a rented New England house, Michael did not even show up at the last minute but we spent a lovely couple of weeks with Gary. The couple and couple thing was obviously not going to work, and gradually we fell out of social contact.

BRUCE NESWICK (USA, WASHINGTON):

I always wondered if Bruce had missed his true vocation. He was an avid church musician and perhaps an even more avid Episcopalian convert, but his background as a Lutheran never faded very far into the past. In cocktail conversation he turned easily and naturally to religion and was always quite sure of himself and his views, although they must have been gleaned largely from undergraduate religion classes at Pacific Lutheran University. I recall with a mixture of amusement and irritation his ready dismissal of my own theological education as he adhered ardently to, in my view, a somewhat simplistic and definitely dogmatic Lutheran line. Was he at heart a Lutheran preacher in Anglican choir robes I wondered to myself? Whatever the case, he is a nice guy and has had an astonishingly brilliant career as the top musician at a succession of important Episcopal cathedrals. I'm told by Charles that Bruce's career as a composer is also flourishing.

JOHN OBETZ (USA, MISSOURI)

John lived one of my big fantasies of promoting the organ as a musical instrument, standing alone with its own musical literature and not just being an accompaniment or church instrument. He had a nationally broadcast radio program called "The Auditorium Organ" which was widely heard and one of the earliest and most successful of its kind. Ironically, as you'd probably guess, it was broadcast from a church anyway; the headquarters in Independence, Missouri, of a group called the Reorganized Church of Jesus

Christ of Latter Day Saints which boasted a 110 rank Aeolian-Skinner organ and good acoustics.

ODILE PIERRE (FRANCE):

We needed to stage a grand party in the large mansion we'd stumbled into in New Jersey and shared with the harpsichordist Robert Edward Smith, because so many folks who supported the cathedral concerts in Newark wanted to see it, and we didn't have time or patience to invite them all individually. In our minds the event amounted a big open house. We also

Our humble little house in New Jersey

thought we may as well get double mileage by using it as a reception for the Parisian organist who was to perform that evening on the Newark cathedral concert series. Our French honoree really did believe the event was all about her, and soon became insufferable to deal with. Some of the French could not only live up to their reputation of being haughty, evidently, but also could be a bit naïve—all too ready to believe the world really did revolve around them.

She later doubled-down on the haughtiness when I got her a featured spot for the only International Congress of Organists ever held in this country. She brought along a male friend, a boyfriend I believe (she was divorced), and used him as a page turner. He ran back and forth behind her to turn alternate pages first from her left and then from her right, etc. I later suggested to her that all of this commotion in the organ balcony was distracting and maybe not a great idea when the audience was able to see it. She responded that French people found homosexuality off-putting. I knew she was intentionally slamming me, but could not figure out the connection to a distracting page turner.

Eventually Odile lost her post at La Madeleine in Paris due to some friction with a priest, as had so many organists in a great variety of settings along the way. Although she had been dismissive of other organists who had suffered a similar fate before her, she now recognized the circumstances as a "tragedy." She proposed rekindling our professional relationship which had concluded some time ago. I made an appointment to talk with her on my next trip to Paris, and found a diminished figure in a simple coat waiting for me in a hotel lobby. The scene was personally compelling, but I decided in the long run that too much time had elapsed since her heyday in the U.S. performance market, and that without her highly recognizable church title the chances of rekindling her previous American touring success was not bright. It was another difficult to absorb lesson in the need to operate the agency as a legitimate business rather than as a sentimental hobby.

JANE PARKER-SMITH (ENGLAND):

Jane stayed with us in the Newark area frequently when on tour gaps or performing on the cathedral series. As a result we were sometimes accidently witnesses to some of the drama in her romantic life—a breakup with her boyfriend in London while our house guest, for example, and the mysterious man who showed up at our door one evening to whisk Jane off on a date after we'd been given just a fifteen minute heads up that she would not be in for dinner (this was long before the ascendancy of e-devices and dating apps).

One evening we took her out to dinner at a fairly upscale Chinese restaurant. We were in the cocktail lounge waiting for our table to be announced when Jane took a fancy to the intricate cork carvings under glass inside the little bar table at which we were seated. In an impulsive move, Jane pulled the glass top aside and reached in, presumably to inspect the fine and delicate workmanship. She emerged with a fist-full of carved cork, seemed a bit stunned for a few seconds like the rest of us, and then tossed the stuff back into the table and pulled the glass top back. Fortunately the results of her investigation were not discovered that night, but John and I never took the chance of returning to that restaurant.

PIERRE PINCEMAILLE (FRANCE):

A fabulous organist and improvisateur but a poster-boy for the 20th century Gallic habit of chain smoking. At the organ bench the ashes from his ubiquitous cigarette fell over his hands and covered the keyboards. If the cigarette got too short before he finished the piece, he would simply place the burning stub on the bench, which, at St. Denis, his post outside Paris, had already suffered a number of resulting scars. I was sad to hear of his early demise, but not overly surprised.

THOMAS RICHNER (USA, WEST VIRGINIA):

Richner, although also an organist, was better known as a pianist, and he was also one of the memorable "characters" who populated our ranks. He was about the same age as his father's second wife, and after his father's death he provided a home for his step-mother for the rest of her life. She, in turn, never stopped being a 'mother figure' who essentially cooked, cleaned, and served as a homemaker for him.

He and Virgil Fox had a sort of tandem shtick going for years as a "you're the best pianist and I'm the best organist" pair, and Virgil used to crawl under Richner's piano and lie on the floor to hear the instrument in what obviously must have been the proper acoustical position. Richner always sprinkled talcum powder on his hands to perform, and if the piano was a baby grand he could be counted on to turn to the audience and say simply, "Baby powder," which always brought the desired reaction.

To me one of the most interesting things about Tom Richner was his love/hate relationship with his born-into religion, Christian Science. He was for long years organist of The First Church of Christ Scientist in Boston, always labeled "the mother church." This position always had him a little on edge because Christian "Scientists" evidently had the propensity of spying on each other to make sure no one was cheating on the "no medical doctors or treatments" dogma of the group. Richner late in life did need medical help and twice had to endure a hospital stay. He was always slightly titillated by this, as though he was a naughty boy who had gotten by unobserved taking a cookie from the jar. But he always swore his friends to absolute silence on the matter because his console at the 'Mother Church' would be jeopardized if word got out to any of the many people evidently waiting to dethrone him.

J. MARCUS RITCHIE (USA, GEORGIA):

He was the 'Southern Gentleman' on the agency roster, albeit a gentleman of rather rakish and liberated ways. It was he who introduced us to the southern custom of the "Dresser," the stiff drink one takes while dressing to go out for an evening of drinking. Marc was one of at least three of our artists along the way to succumb to complications of the HIV/AIDS virus which left many holes in organist ranks in the latter 20th century.

MCNEIL ROBINSON (USA, ALABAMA):

The long-time organist of the legendary Church of St. Mary the Virgin near Times Square, McNeil was given to relying on an array of exotic medicines and potions and carried an assortment of them in a leather bag whenever he travelled. Arriving by train in Hartford to perform at Trinity College he somehow forgot to take the bag with him and it rode on alone to the end of the line in Springfield, Massachusetts. So Neil went to Trinity to make friends with the organ, while I returned to the station to retrieve his bag of chemicals when the train got back to Hartford on its return trip. It turned out, however, that Neil had stashed his electronic metronome in the bag with all the chemical cures. When the train reached Springfield, something set off the metronome, passengers suspected a bomb, and the police were called. There were police at the station in Hartford waiting for the same bag I had been sent to collect, because it had brought out the bomb squad when it was discovered in Springfield.

After being reunited with his bag, and having sufficient initial keyboard time, Neil went to dinner with us at a nice place in the courtyard of an apartment building where my harpsichordist Robert Edward Smith lived.

For whatever reason John had complained at table about something minor like being a little tired. McNeil snapped into evangelical mode for his varied chemical cures, and was sure he had just the right thing for John right here in his bag. He whipped out a bottle and insisted John must try it. Out of politeness, but certainly not for medical reasons, John took a small sip of the concentrated Niacin.

Soon I was staring across the table at my partner as his eyes rolled backwards and he slumped onto the table. Sure that I was losing him, I shouted in the restaurant for someone to call an ambulance and then raced across the courtyard to the lobby of Robert's apartment building. The doorman phoned up to Robert and I collapsed from terror onto the lobby floor.

By the time the ambulance was ready to whisk John off to the ER, Robert had come over to the restaurant to sit with Neil. Eventually both John and I survived the ordeal and I returned to the restaurant where Neil and Robert were still sitting at table. Why are you still here, I asked, as much to have anything to say at all under the circumstances. "Because I can't stand up," the organist answered. "When John fainted I thought he was dying and peed my pants. It's still not dry."

But wait, there's more, as the TV adv'ts scream. When Neil finally got to the organ console he discovered he'd packed two left-foot organ shoes instead of a pair. I submitted the whole adventure to a gossip columnist at our local daily newspaper (there still were such animals at that stage of American life) and we captured some ink for the Trinity College organ series. Are organists somehow a bit different from ordinary mortals? It makes one wonder.

JOHN ROSE (USA, GEORGIA):

John appears here and there throughout this account because he is my life partner and was also a business partner. But in addition he was an artist represented for many years by my agency and the only one of our performers ever to be hospitalized while on tour. After a performance in Wisconsin at an abbey where he was given a guest room, he awoke the next morning in pain. He attempted breakfast with the monks, but soon realized he had to reluctantly ask for help. Then he was being whisked off to a local hospital in an ambulance for attention to what turned out to be a kidney stone. The boy certainly knew how to make a dramatic exit.

He once, the day before flying to a recital city, called ahead to the church to arrange practice hours on the organ. The secretary who answered his call looked at her log and advised him that there was no recital scheduled—and that the church musician who had signed our booking agreement had been committed to a mental hospital weeks ago. The agency shifted procedure henceforth and required a clergy signature on all performance contracts.

John's road-warrior stories are far too numerous for this space, but they range over the same territory organists and non-organist performers must face. He once landed in Montgomery AL, for a scheduled performance only to find the airport swarming with state troopers and everyone in an obvious panic. He and his fellow passengers could not have known that George Wallace had been shot just minutes ago, and that two of the Governor's children were still unaccounted for with theories of a plot against the family making the rounds.

Travel can be its own trial for musicians, as when John once had to take five separate flights and land to change planes at four different airports to get between back-to-back recitals in Regina, Saskatchewan, Canada, and Salem OR. Then there were the critics, often the bane of any performer. More than once John found himself a football in the ego wars of local critics, with a glowing review in the morning paper refuted point by point in a scalding evening paper review. Of course, performers today don't really have to worry about that much anymore because there are fewer and fewer newspapers around, and fewer and fewer critics writing for them—in my opinion a significant loss.

But one did not always even have to leave home for the bizarre twist. John's late nighttime practicing (often the only time of day feasible in a busy building) at Sacred Heart Cathedral in Newark was often accompanied by the sound of footsteps in the organ chambers where, the legend was, one of the cathedral builders had fallen to his death.

JOHN SCOTT (ENGLAND):

If one of my artists was ever the 'proper English gentleman' it was John Scott, although I think his family background was not especially high in the rigid English social system nor do I recall that he had a "public school" education, as the strange English euphemism has it. He unfailingly hosted me for dinner whenever I was in London on business, usually with his wife at a restaurant near their home in the close of St. Paul's Cathedral where he was assistant music director before taking on the top job himself. The only time I heard him say anything which might be challenged on the measure of gentlemanliness was at the reception celebrating his succession to the top music job at St. Paul's. His predecessor had retired to New Zealand (I'm pretty sure it was) where, John Scott told the party gathering, the predecessor and his wife had promptly become nudists. "It gives new meaning to the term 'organ buff,'" he said as part of his remarks.

Obviously that was just a stab at a bit of humor to enliven the proceedings, but I've always felt it was somewhat unworthy of John Scott's perpetual courtesy and dignity. For example, one evening when I had flown to the Chicago area to hear one of his tour performances we were having a drink in the hotel lobby and I noticed that he had finished his drink while I was nursing mine. He waited patiently until I'd finished to announce that he was ready for bed, and I suddenly realized his English manners would not allow him to leave while I was still drinking.

His divorce may have been the most defining event in his life. Despite his great reserve and taciturn inclination, he told me, "I don't understand why it was necessary," leaving the threads of a complicated plot dangling somewhat enticingly in mid-air. When he moved to New York City to head the music program at St. Thomas Church, Fifth Avenue, he was, to my eyes, a different man. To my observation there had been an obvious personality change, and a new bitterness and cold pragmatism had replaced his previous gentle spirit. By the time of his second marriage I'd lost track of him. I hope it brought a renewal of happiness. I can't help but suspect, however, that the pain and profound sorrow of that divorce stayed with him to his untimely death.

ROBERT EDWARD SMITH (USA, NEW JERSEY):

Robert (nobody ever called him "Bob;" he was about as far from a diminutive as one could get) was a church organist but performed on stage only as a harpsichordist. For several years in New Jersey he and John and I were housemates in a lovely many-roomed mansion that we had stumbled upon at a ridiculous bank clearance price, but could only afford by throwing in our lots with each other. We had a large 'music room' which never held a stick of furniture beyond his unusually big nine-foot harpsichord, and the rest of the great house was fairly lightly furnished as well, owing to church musician level salaries coupled with monthly thousand-plus dollar winter heating bills.

Robert's many talents included handiness in the kitchen and he became the *de facto* chef of the household. At some point my parents and my aunt and uncle drove to New Jersey from Iowa for a visit, and Robert whipped up his signature chicken-rice-lemon dish. We sat around a table too small for the dining room with its great stone fireplace, and enjoying our share of wine along with Robert's chicken *ala* lemon. At some point late in the meal the three locals noticed that my "eccentric" uncle Scotty had thrown his paper napkin on his plate and that it was now disappearing forkful by forkful. After looking at each other with a "did you see what I saw?" shock, Robert graciously offered, "Scotty, would you like another napkin?" Scotty, equally gracious, accepted and proceeded to eat the next napkin as well. Fortunately the big house had kept us poor enough that we had not yet graduated to cloth napkins.

This house had a big yard and was the first residence that John and I had lived in together without the confines of an apartment. For us, that meant we needed a dog. We had grown up with a parade of dogs each; Robert had grown up in the most densely populated state in the country without such pleasures. I decided to surprise my housemates by taking the matter into my own hands, and reward them, after they returned from some event at Newark cathedral, with a lovely Irish setter puppy. John was totally thrilled. Robert *said* he was thrilled.

Puppies, of course, need to be house trained. Robert's intuition told him that when our puppy had an accident on the kitchen floor, the proper response was to grab the dog and throw him into the pantry and slam the door shut—for long enough to teach him a lesson. For some reason the dog never figured out what Robert's point was, and eventually I gave up and gave him to a family with small children where he and the kids proceeded to flourish. Much later in Connecticut when John and I had another yard, and thus another dog, Robert came over for dinner. "I just can't understand why people want to have a dog in the house," he announced. "It's like having a brain damaged child under foot." Robert was always ready with a pithy line, mostly by calculation I suspect.

Lest I leave you with an entirely erroneous impression of Robert let me hasten to say that he has a big heart and can be as compassionate as anyone you'd care to meet; he just had never had the chance to love a pet. Later, however, he did manage to coexist with a cat for a few months. In a PTCA newsletter interview he responded to a question about pets: "I'm sorry, but I find it impossible to understand why one would choose to share one's home with a creature who is not only incapable of serious conversation, but who insists on being led by the neck, naked, into the street rather than learn how to use the toilet. I suppose tropical fish are all right. I don't have any."

HERNDON SPILLMAN (USA, LOUISIANA):

I got an early lesson in emerging American feminism when I once telephoned Herndon at home. "May I speak with Dr. Spillman," I asked the female answering voice. "Well, *WHICH* 'Dr. Spillman' do you want to speak with?," she answered, obviously somewhat peeved. Herndon's wife, like him, was a highly educated professor at Louisiana State University. Herndon had a special place on the American organ scene as perhaps the most prominent black musician in our midst, or at least one of the most prominent and earliest. He'd studied in France and then spent his career zoned somewhat narrowly in on his French teacher, the composer Maurice Duruflé.

ERNST-ERICH STENDER (GERMANY):

Once at dinner with this German organist and his wife, I noticed I was avoiding addressing her because I didn't know her first name and wasn't sure of the German custom or how it worked—first name as we would address another adult here, or something with a particular German twist? Without a smile she replied, "You can call me 'Mrs. Stender.'" Case closed.

DANIEL SULLIVAN & HEIDI EMMERT (WISCONSIN & GERMANY):

These two unrelated performers had in common being very good at their art, but also having relatives who ultimately forced them to abandon their performance careers. Heidi's parents objected to her touring even though her career was flourishing and she kept winning one performance competition after another. I think they feared for her financial future, although I was never given an explanation with much detail. She ended up taking a low-profile teaching post for school-aged children that her father, or her uncle, had once held, and thus her wings were safely clipped because she could not be absent to tour.

Dan's family belonged to a tiny Lutheran sect in Wisconsin which believed that even other Lutherans were heretics. His father was an official of some kind in that group. It had been drilled into Dan that it was sinful to pray with anyone outside their own little group, as he explained it, "or risk my eternal soul." If a recital presenter wanted to have a short prayer led by the pastor before a church recital, as happened all too frequently for my taste, Dan would have to leave the building and then return after the prayer was safely finished. Finally there was just too much pressure from home, and Dan acquiesced to the only real option he had—he just turned his back on performing. When I last heard of him, he was working in a fast-food chain restaurant and teaching piano lessons, if memory serves.

So two gifted young organists lost their dreams to unrelenting family pressure, and the concert organ scene lost two outstanding young performers who, in my judgement, would have contributed significantly to the field.

TRINITY COLLEGE CHOIR (CAMBRIDGE, ENGLAND)

Like all of the great English university choirs this ensemble was so well coached and consistently excellent through wave after wave of student members that the only anecdotes come from the fringes of working with them. In Trinity's case, it's a memory of a phone call with the director, the late Richard Marlow. I'd been warned about the tricky pronunciations of English place names by Nicolas Kynaston and was always leery of embarrassing myself by letting slip an American version. It was Marlow, however, who tipped me off that American place names could also pose a problem to the English. When the choir was on tour here he needed to call in from the road once to ask about arrangements at its next stop in Illinois. Being a Midwesterner myself, I instinctively knew how we Americans properly say "pee-**OR**-i-a." When Marlow phoned in, he asked me about

Glancing Back

the arrangements in "pee-a-**REE**-a." I've had trouble since then trying to disconnect the city from images of men's rooms.

ROBERT TWYNHAM (USA, MARYLAND)

Twynham, an early member of our roster, was a gifted musician with an impressive post: The modernistic (Catholic) Cathedral of Mary Our Queen in Baltimore, Maryland. He had studied with Messiaen and therefore quite logically decided to play the composer's "Nativity Suite" before a Christmas Eve Mass one year. The Cardinal evidently had somewhat different musical tastes, however, and after Mass he stormed up to the organ loft and ordered Twynham never to "play that man's music in my cathedral again." Robert did comply—until the Cardinal died. Then, at the Cardinal's funeral, he played *nothing but* Messiaen!

This is the same cathedral church, by the way, at which Virgil Fox, arriving the first night to prepare for a recital, walked to the edge of the organ loft and surveyed the scene: "Mary, Honey, you've got a gorgeous temple," he shouted into the empty nave. (He probably did it to gauge the acoustics, but Virgil was not one to waste any opportunity to be outrageous at the same time.)

JOHN WALKER (USA, PENNSYLVANIA)

John graciously interviewed me for a TAO feature article a few months after my retirement from PTCA (Appendix 2), so let's turn the table on him and have a look at a few of his answers to an interview published many years ago in the PTCA newsletter.

Favorite simple (non-commercial) pleasure?: "Chocolate and anything related to it."

Pet(s)?: "At the moment I have no pets. But I keep remembering a wonderful little dog, a Lhasa Maltese, which was named Herbie in honor of my organ professor, Herbert Nanney. I think that Professor Nanney was honored by this, but I have never been quite certain."

What led to your choice of instrument?: "Having lost my practice discipline on the piano, I elected to study oboe in junior high school. But I could not find the real desire to practice that instrument either. After a year of begging and solemn promises to mend my ways, I convinced my parents that they should invest in organ study for me during high school. As luck had it, our church organist became ill that year, allowing me to fill in for several weeks. The opportunity to play in services confirmed my wish (and need) to practice!"

Several of the organists we represented were active on the national level of the AGO, but John was the only one to reach its presidency.

JANE WATTS (ENGLAND):

Throughout my agency career husbands played a big role in trying to get us to represent their wives as performers, sometimes respectfully and sometimes like they were wielding a club, but always with admirable, if sometimes frustrating, persistence. Jane Watts' husband was a refreshing exception to the rule—not an exception in terms of persistence, but in terms of lacking any hint of bullying, and of his being out front himself in doing whatever could be done towards the goal. His devotion to her was heart-warming, although I was never quite sure which of them really coveted the performer's role more, she, or he on her behalf. He had two jobs of his own during the period I knew them, first as an assistant to an English agent for organists, as I recall, and then as an executive at a recording label. Both jobs were undertaken, I have little doubt, because of his devotion to Jane and his search for any way to advance her performance career.

MARIANNE WEBB (AMERICAN, KANSAS):

She came to us with a long career as a reasonably prominent performer already under her belt, but slipping and hoping for a career revival. A lot of good things followed, but her career never revived to the extent either she or I wished for. She bequeathed to the AGO funds to program an event at every subsequent national convention at which the entire convention could be present at the same time (often churches with good instruments are small enough that a convention has to divide the audience into shifts).

Marianne was always cheerful and nice to be around, but was also very much a 'character' who defied a quick or conventional profile. She maintained in her home in Carbondale, Illinois, a living room into which every guest was afraid to step, and in fact into which they were never invited to step—white carpet, white sofas covered in heavy clear plastic, and all-around the aesthetics of a hospital surgery room.

Late in life she decided to divorce her husband, a fellow faculty member. "You just have no idea what it's like to be married to a gay man," she told me. Well, true, since my partner and I were not yet legally eligible for marriage at that time. But I don't think her husband was, in fact, gay, and later evidence would support my analysis. He was, however, unfailingly kind and helpful to her after their divorce as she aged and struggled with her terminal illness.

Marianne is another of my artists from along the way from whom I carry a tagline. "Oh, Phil, you're *sooooo* distinguished," she was fond of telling me every time we met at yet another AGO convention. Unfortunately John and Ray were frequently nearby as witnesses, so now when I least expect it, I have another "Oh, Phil, you're *sooooo* distinguished!"

thrown my way—probably now delivered in irony or sarcasm rather than admiration.

GILLIAN WEIR (NEW ZEALAND, TRANSPLANTED TO ENGLAND):

The location of her birth seemed to be almost a defining, and challenging, character in her story and she seemed to be always running from it. The closest explanation I was ever given by her was that people, especially the English, tended to assume that if one was from New Zealand, one was actually an Australian, and to be an Australian was to be a somewhat crude rube. Eventually she achieved an honor which would appear to have given her the longed-for status she craved in England. She told the story eagerly to me at dinner in London years after we had severed our professional affiliation—the party for the inductees on the grounds of Buckingham Palace, the drama and ritual surrounding the investiture by the Queen, and the pride of being "Dame Gillian Weir." But the victory had feet of clay—New Zealand clay. She was not on the honors list of England, but of her home country, where her brother was a wealthy businessman of significant political clout.

Not long after becoming what to American eyes seemed almost like minor royalty, she was pulled over by the police while driving home to suburban Redding (England). The story was a bit murky in the telling, probably understandably, but the gist seemed to be that Gillian identified herself with the "Dame" title which set off the policeman into a stiff lecture on how that did not get her off the hook for speeding, or anything else for that matter, and even worse, the venting of a lot of pent-up social strata frustrations by a 'lower class' cop. Her new title was hollow and instead of ridding her of the chains of New Zealand, actually just tightened them.

Gillian always had dedicated fans, including one business man who once walked the sixty miles between London and Oxford to hear her perform (part of a fund-raising effort for the restoration of an historic English pipe organ).

BRADLEY WELCH (USA, TEXAS):

Bradley became one of the prize winner sources of tension between McFarlane and PTCA, although the details are a touch hazy to me at this point. He won the third round of the Dallas International Organ Performance Competition, which included representation by us. But, as I recall, he had already qualified as a finalist in the next national AGO competition, the winner of which would get automatic McFarlane representation. What I'm not sure of anymore is the exact sequence of the story. In any case Bradley was left to decide on a sure thing by accepting our offer, or to wait and gamble on winning the AGO—at least that's as close as I can come to reconstructing the timeline. In any case, the McFarlane opportunity at the time of the mini-fight was only a potential which still depended on Bradley actually winning at the AGO convention.

Karen was not in the slightest pleased, and seemed to feel that by merely entering the AGO competition Bradley had already made a commitment to her agency in case he were to win. Karen asked her artist who was the chief organ professor at Yale, where Bradley was then a student, to intervene and things were beginning to get a bit ugly with some colorful language entering the picture. I decided to withdraw my offer to Bradley for the sake of world peace and harmony. When he did not win the AGO competition in question, he ended up on our roster after all by virtue of the Dallas win. Whenever I think of Bradley, despite his talent, poise, and gentlemanliness, I can't help thinking of Karen's inventive description of him when she felt her toes were being stepped on. I was somewhat shocked, too, that the mere potential of winning a prize was being viewed as a commitment to a specific agency, as though the winner would be honor-bound to accept the representation offered, and thus should be deprived of an earlier "bird in the hand" choice.

Bradley had taken a church musician's position in Dallas before winning the competition there, and ended up spending his career in the city. He is now organist of the Dallas Symphony Orchestra, succeeding another of our PTCA artists, Mary Preston.

JOHN SCOTT WHITELY (ENGLAND, ASSISTANT MUSICIAN YORK MINSTER):

Although he toured in the U.S. a number of times and was featured in a significant long running television series in the U.K. as an organ recitalist, I remember him most vividly from a tiny vignette in the York Minster close. We had been invited to lunch at the head organist's house when he discovered he had not stocked in any wine for the occasion. Off went JSW to his own apartment and emerged carrying a bottle across the quad. "Rescuing Sherry" he announced. This became another of the many refrains we picked up from various artists which are now engrained into our household argot. A bottle of almost anything on almost any occasion can now suddenly become "rescuing sherry."

MALCOLM WILLIAMSON (AUSTRALIA):

Malcolm cannot be contained or even hinted at in the confines of a couple of paragraphs. It would take an entire very large book just to give a surface gloss to this incredible musician and composer, and irrepressible personality, from Australia, who for many years until his death was "Master of the Queen's Music" to HM Elizabeth II of England (and the British Commonwealth).

Glancing Back

My last memory of him, which came many years after we no longer worked together, was from inside a rail car sitting on the track in a small English town preparing for departure. I had just had dinner with Malcolm and his partner at their home in this English backwater, and they were seeing me off at the station. I'd found a seat and settled in, when a rather nice looking student-appearing guy took a seat in my otherwise empty row. Suddenly, there was Malcolm tapping on the window from the outside and shaking his finger at me in mock admonition to behave myself. Malcolm would never have failed to notice a scene of potential like that, even if he had already left the station and had to reappear by magic.

Malcolm was simply an incorrigible people-lover and could not stop himself from engaging anyone and everyone in conversation. A simple cup of coffee with him would inevitably lead to a few steps into the life of a stranger. I remember once in Newark when our waitress wore a name tag saying, "Hello, I'm Millie." Malcolm wanted to know what kind of a name "Imallie" was, and we were off to the races chatting with a woman caught as off guard as was I. On the wider stage Malcolm was just as fearless and outspoken. After his appointment as Master of the Queen's Music, during a national BBC radio interview he referred to then British Prime Minister Margaret Thatcher as a "mindless philistine," who had done more to hurt cultural life than any other British leader since World War II, a comment then widely reported by the international press.

Malcolm and my relationship was professional rather than personal, but with Malcolm it would have been impossible for any relationship not to have been personal, even close, as well. With him, "bigger than life" was not a cliché, it was a modest description. I was aware of one of the few things which Malcolm allowed to cause him sadness, however. He was a really gung-ho Roman Catholic who had married into a Jewish family, and did not try to hide the fact that it bothered him greatly that his children were not baptized.

21 Flavor of the Scene

There are a few things about fans of the organ which I still don't quite understand even after all these years of living amongst them; a half-century evidently is just not enough time to figure out all of the quirkiness our scene encouraged.

For example, why did some die-hard fans attach themselves **exclusively** to organ music? I've known some who were simply totally uninterested in any other musical genre. And often these folks were real gluttons who just couldn't get enough, and may have devoted an entire retirement to chasing down and attending every single organ recital they could learn about. I'm not just referring to one or two people or couples; I've known several directly. And these rabid fans were usually not organists themselves, but converts from some ecstatic experience along the way. I have my musical favorites too, but come on folks; refusing to listen to anything except organ music is just plain weird.

And these organ super-fans were often convinced that the whole world shared (or should share) their passion. One retired couple stands out in memory for buying the same organ recordings over and over again at never-to-be-missed recitals. "Sign this one for Aunt Sue," they'd instruct the performer in the reception line. "This one's for Sam next door. And sign this one 'Happy Birthday, Alice'." I have no doubt many of the recipients were surprised by the generosity of the organ fans, and I have no doubt either that many of these recordings ended up somewhere other than the LP shelf.

Then there were the diehard fans, often not themselves organists either, who might actually have been willing to skip the music altogether. Their interest seemed to be largely confined to the instrument and its mechanics, and many of them may have been just as maniacal about model trains or street trolleys as they were about the organ. They flocked to OHS (and maybe ATOS) conventions to be with their own kind, and attend recitals for which they stood and whooped and hollered regardless of who performed, how well he performed, what was performed, what the instrument was, or any other considerations which more rational audiences might take into account. For these folks, happy bedtime reading could be a long stop-list from an obscure instrument in a far-away place by an unknown builder.

Eventually we come to the organists themselves, so many of whom in my day seemed enthralled with the idea of sitting on a bench as if *rigor mortis* had already set in, not moving a muscle anywhere in their bodies except their fingers (and sometimes the moving fingers were not even allowed to include their thumbs). They had to sit rigidly straight and stare at the always present score on the music rack, while not giving the slightest hint that the music actually moved them emotionally in the slightest. Maybe it didn't! The music they made was seldom infectious, but we were assured that it was being at least *correctly* made, which took precedence over enjoyment if one were a true, legitimate, organist. My own observation was that the organists who were moved by the music themselves were the most successful at communicating its beauty to others, and when the organist did feel the music he couldn't avoid some movement beyond that which was strictly necessary to press or pedal the keys. (Thank every god in the sky that the young organists of the current century seem to have kicked those *rigor mortis* habits. Young organists today are also boldly performing the dreaded transcriptions so many were told they must deny themselves last century.)

And on that note, why was the organ so militantly assigned to the category "religion" rather than the category "music", not only by the general public, but by so many organists themselves. I've complained about that several times above, but need to insert a mini-rant again here because I still don't understand; and I still think organists thereby were short-changing themselves. It's surely okay to be religious and an organist at the same time, but if hymn playing is regarded as the apex of the organist's art, something is seriously wrong.

So there were mysteries hidden from me during my long sojourn with the organists. But I loved the music they made, especially when they weren't playing hymns, and I learned to love a great many of them as personalities, albeit sometimes as perhaps "interesting" personalities. (Of course, I suppose it's possible I may have contributed an "interesting" aspect or two along the way myself.)

One thing which can safely be said about the organ as a musical instrument, however, is that its reach has been very long. One of the most ubiquitous descriptive phrases used in the English language is "Pull(ing/ed/s) out all the stops." Almost everyone has used the phrase from time to time whether they understand what it means, or where it came from, or not. So the organ has to some extent permeated our culture even if it has become largely invisible to many along the way.

Organists & Me

One of my chief career frustrations was the meekness with which organists seemed to accept their perceived status of living on the fringe of the legitimate concert scene. They seemed not to care very much that most people thought the word "church" was permanently attached to the words "organ" and "organist." Most of them seemed content to perform only for Sunday morning congregations, or for those same people in an occasional recital in the same building. Maybe, in fairness, that was a survival mechanism for many of these good (and talented) people. They got to ply their art, at least to a degree, and they got paid for it. To do the same outside a church was a major difficulty requiring iron fortitude and at least a degree of good fortune. The concert scene had pretty much consigned organists to its bottom rung, depriving them gradually of settings in which to perform and of money in any significant amount in payment for performing. So church became a safe haven and organists started to forget that they and their instrument had such a grand performance history on stage, and so much potential to engage, entertain, and inspire a wider audience. They forgot that the organ was the "king" of instruments and settled for it being the mere chaplain of instruments.

This problem then became a self-fulfilling prophecy which gradually ate away not only at the number of performers who could devote the time and effort needed for the concert stage, but also at their potential audiences who were being told by example and implication that organ was on an inferior level to voice or violin or orchestra. This insularity was largely enforced on the organist scene from the outside, but the organists, as a community, were also too compliant in accepting it. The encouragement I feel at this point is that many young organists are less meek in accepting the idea of living on the fringe, and are much more determined to make inroads into the main event.

22 A Note in Parting

Thanks to the organists who let me come and play in their sand box with them for so many years. I sometimes felt like a kid from the wrong side of the tracks who was accepted anyway.

I just hope I left something useful behind. I'd like to think I stood for, and furthered, the cause of the pipe organ standing alone as a legitimate concert instrument without necessarily being tied to the church. What I did contribute was, at least, helping to keep the art of organ performance viable through another generation or two before handing it off to the vagaries of the future. But perhaps ironically, most of the many hundreds of organ recitals I attended during this career did take place in churches. The organ is likely to remain tied to church (assuming 2020 and the virus don't alter our world too radically) but I just don't want the organ to be completely swallowed by church. The organ has more to offer, and more musical potential, than merely serving as an ecclesiastical accompaniment instrument.

The organ performance scene is a brutally tough market. It's overcrowded with talent (a bright spot in and of itself) and too small to absorb all of that talent, at least in the aspect of professional level performance fees. Our market during my time was a classic case of supply significantly exceeding demand, and that meant there was always an overlay of frustration for both performers and agents. I want to believe this imbalance can resolve itself without subtracting some of the talent, and several new concert halls with new pipe organs yield a little apparent hope in that direction. But other forces are at work too, especially the decline of traditional organized Christianity which is closing church structures at a frightening clip today (beginning well before 2020 and its virus), robbing the organ scene not only of instruments but of communities of people to serve as presenters. We're beginning to observe talented young organists dropping out of the scene to look for other areas of work, and the closing of some long established university organ departments bears foreboding witness to the process.

So it's obvious that the art of organ performance is going to evolve in appearance and structure, and that the future will likely look increasingly unlike the past which I now represent, or the models I helped to survive a bit longer. My day was somewhere in the not-easy-to-define transition from the Age of Pisces (the age that began at the time of Jesus and contained the Christian era) to the Age of Aquarius (which is likely to embrace a totally different world outlook and religious expression; the signs are already too numerous to list). So change is coming, whether we're ready for it, or happy about it, or not.

Two quick notes about this book:

A) My original conception was to write basically a history of the agency up to my retirement. My peer group readers/proofers asked for more detail about me and my personal journey into the realm of the organ. Thus the book became a combination of memoir, agency history, and short essays on the field from my perspective. I hope I got the balance right, and apologize if parts seem to focus too much on my own journey.

B) After I was essentially finished writing this, I put the book aside for a period to regain a less intense perspective than the initial writing had called for. During that time we all experienced the Covid-19 crisis and much about our lives changed. Inevitably the organ scene will change along with the rest of life. Rather than trying to predict the future of the organ as a performance instrument, which is far beyond my capacity at this point in any case, I decided simply to let this book stand as a reflection of where we had been as an organ community for roughly half a century before 2020.

And two quick hopes for the AGO:

A) The AGO needs to, and I have no doubt will, continue to serve the interests and needs of church organists. But it needs to remain a big tent also, serving the interests and needs of organists and people connected with the organ who are there for non-church reasons too. These people have no other organizational home, and it's really up to the AGO to keep them from becoming organizational orphans. That's not an easy assignment, but well worth the effort if the good of the organ and its music is the paramount goal.

B) The AGO will also need to fight the temptation to become just an exercise in self-preservation, especially as membership numbers tighten. Keeping the doors open, as it were, is a good thing only if the organization continues to serve the causes it was created for. Merely continuing to exist is not the goal, or at least shouldn't be.

The future of the organ as a performance instrument may not be in as *many* hands as it was when I jumped into the field, but I believe (and *need* to believe) that it is in *good* hands. Hands like those of Christopher Houlihan to whom I've dedicated this memoir because of his stunning accomplishments before age thirty, his equally great promise during his ensuing mature decades, and his great gift to me of being able to feel that my life's work really did help yield something of value to the future. So I have to leave it to

A Note in Parting

the young organists now; I don't have any other choice. But I'm optimistic in the face of serious challenges because I know a lot of these young guys and gals in the field, and they are not only brilliant but also resourceful enough to put up a good fight on behalf of the musical instrument we all love equally.

Appendix 1: Cast of Abbreviated Characters

AGO: The American Guild of Organists, a New York based organization for church musicians, not quite a labor union and not quite not a union either. Despite its name, it seemed to me often to be dominated by choral interest and interests to a greater extent than by organ interests. Its membership consisted of full-time professional church musicians, whether organists or choir directors, or both, plus a lot of part-time church musicians of various levels of accomplishment and a scattering of folks whose involvement with the organ was simply that of addicted fans. Most of the organists in either category considered themselves recital caliber musicians, and some actually were.

The first time I served on the host committee for an AGO regional convention I complained at one meeting that there were so many choral events on the planned program, and so few organ events. "But choir is what we do," explained a fellow committee member, obviously confused that I couldn't seem to figure that out on my own. When I first began working as an agent for organists, the AGO membership stood in the area of 28,000 if memory serves. As I write this it stands at around 11,000. The AGO worries about its future as an organization, and most of its members worry about the future of the organ performance art form and church music as a profession.

AAM: Association of Anglican [Church] Musicians. A sort of mini-AGO, but especially for Episcopalians.

ALCM: Association of Lutheran Church Musicians. A sort of mini-AGO, but especially for Lutherans.

APAP: Association of Performing Arts Presenters (presenters of anything and everything musical as long as it isn't organ).

ASCAP: American Society of Composers, Authors and Publishers. A copyright protection organization which sells licenses to perform material not yet in the public domain.

ASOFH: Albert Schweitzer Organ Festival Hartford (the "H" was added a couple of decades into the life of the festival). A competition for young organists and a performance festival held annually (except

Appendix 1

in 2020 because of the virus) at Trinity College in Hartford, Connecticut.

ATOS: American Theatre Organ Society. A sort of AGO for non-organists and organists alike, albeit with significant differences in instruments and repertoire.

CMA: Chamber Music America, an organization of presenters.

"HOULI": Christopher Houlihan, as in "Houli-Fans."

ICO: International Congress of Organists, an occasional gathering of organ types from Europe and North America sponsored by the AGO, RCO, and RCCO, and defunct for many years.

INS: Immigration and Naturalization Service of the United States in charge of issuing visas for foreign performers to tour in the U.S., or, in the case of organists, pointing out that they are not as famous as rock stars. Now called USCIS.

ISPA: International Society of Performing Arts Presenters

JOHN: Unless otherwise specified my (after the Supreme Court ruling) husband. He's now retired after over a half century in the music field, first as cathedral organist in Newark and then for four decades as College Organist and professor at Trinity College, Hartford. He had a performance career which took him to four continents. His chief pride now is his many students who have distinguished themselves in music and other fields, including and especially the prominent American concert organist Christopher Houlihan who succeeded him at Trinity College. [Just before this book was published, John's retirement from Trinity College ended when he was called back to become interim Director of Spiritual and Religious Life on campus. This was a Dean's level position, but the rules didn't allow an interim appointment to carry the designation of 'Dean,' so John continues to be known to students as 'Mr. Rose,' and very rarely as Prof. Rose, which while accurate seldom seemed to fit the friendly dynamic between John and his students.]

Appendix 1

NYT: *The New York Times* newspaper, the grand old lady of American journalism. Despite an occasional fly landing on her once in a while, she is still the best paper our country (or the world) has to offer.

OHS: The Organ Historical Society, a group which could become as excited by the instrument itself as by the music being played on it.

PTCA: Phillip Truckenbrod Concert Artists, which began life known as 'Arts Image' and constituted my adult career.

RAY: Unless otherwise specified my primary business partner in the agency who became essentially an adopted son to John and me and with whom we still share our Hartford house. After the agency was taken over by Charles Miller, Ray continued on in the organ field and is now an organ builder for the venerable Austin Organ Company.

RCO: Royal College of Organists, a UK organization similar to the AGO and upon which the AGO was mostly modeled.

RCCO: Royal Canadian College of Organists, the AGO north of the border.

TAO: *The American Organist*, a monthly journal published by the AGO. Despite being totally dependent on volunteer writers (the AGO actually depended on TAO for its own organizational income by way of its value to advertisers) this journal actually was one of the country's important musical publications in its heyday. Before becoming TAO it was named simply *Music*. When I launched the agency its editor was Peter J. Basch, who worked from a little office in midtown Manhattan. By the time of his successor Charles Henderson the AGO had set up shop in the Interchurch Building in upper Manhattan and the journal moved along with it. My friend Tony Baglivi was the longtime editor of considerable legend and is still on the masthead as "editor emeritus."

USCIS: United States Customs and Immigration Service, the agents in charge of being pains-in-the-neck about giving entry visas to foreign performers, especially organists. In my day known as INS.

Appendix 2: TAO Interview

TAO INTERVIEW OF PHILLIP TRUCKENBROD BY JOHN WALKER, PUBLISHED IN THE SEPTEMBER 2016 ISSUE:

John Walker: First I want to congratulate you upon your successful completion of a 50 year career in active concert management. That must be some sort of record for longevity in this profession! Yes?
Phil Truckenbrod: I think so. However I need to correct your number. It's 48 years. I had planned to last as long as 50 or more years, but in order to get Charles Miller to step in to lead the agency, a two year adjustment needed to be made between my goal and the circumstances which would allow him to take the position.

Interestingly, perhaps, Karen McFarlane and I started in this field at almost exactly the same time—she organizing a small agency in Texas before taking over for Lillian Murtagh. Then our careers paralleled each other for decades until her retirement some years ago. I've lost count of the number of times a message for one of us ended up in the other's in-box.

Q: Is there a story behind your initial choice of "Arts Image" as the name of your agency?
A: Not an especially interesting one. We originally planned to operate equally as a public relations agency for arts organizations (I was arts writer for the country's seventh largest daily newspaper at the time) and an agency for performers. The latter just took over.

Q: What has been most gratifying, most rewarding, in those nearly five decades?
A: Amid many pleasures along the way, I'd need to say it was helping young performers emerge into significant careers. This was especially true when the performer went from being almost unknown to having a big breakout career and becoming a major name in the field. Two examples of whom I'm especially proud are Paul Jacobs and Christopher Houlihan, as well as some non-organist performers such as ensemble Amarcord.

Q: Might you perhaps care to elaborate upon your thoughts and experiences in guiding young artists to formation of concert careers?

Appendix 2

A: In the early days of my work the premium was always on foreign performers, who not only seemed to appeal more to American presenters but were widely assumed to be superior to home-grown talent. During my career the tide has turned almost completely, and today we Americans are justly proud of our own performers and the stunning quality of our emerging performers. I'm not claiming credit for this—I'm just saying it was a thrill to be working in the field during this adjustment and to perhaps have made some contributions to it.

Q: What advice would you give to brilliant organ students today who might aspire toward careers in performance?
A: Assuming the student has talent and training to an adequate degree, I think the next big challenge is building name recognition. Today's students have a wide range of social media to work with and can be very clever in building reputations without spending too much money [in the process]. And by all means word of mouth is always the best endorsement.

It's a quirk of human psychology that a familiar name in a given field will be seen as more impressive and talented than an unfamiliar one. Step one is to capitalize on that; to buy into the club, as it were, so that audiences will instinctively feel you have something special to offer. Of course, then you do have to offer something special. I'm not saying you can bluff your way, just that in order to be given a real chance to prove yourself you do need some degree of perceived standing in the field.

The talent certainly needs to be there, and yet talent alone will not make a career. The performer's personality needs to connect with audiences and a wide variety of other people who will influence or control aspects of the performance career. A good stage presence either needs to be naturally present, or consciously developed. Then there's raw good luck, and the ability to attract people along the way who can be helpful, whether a mentor, an agent, or a patron.

I look at a performance career as a lot of hard work, which needs an exceptional amount of commitment.

Q: What criteria have you utilized for selection of artists for your concert roster?
A: Not to make a complex subject seem simple, but if I spotted a performer who seemed to me headed for a significant performance career whether I was a big fan or not, then I usually thought I'd rather have that person on my roster than not. Signs of deep ambition, determination, and inventiveness are all big pluses, and the lack of those qualities is a performing career formula for failure. Sure, we've all observed performers

Appendix 2

whose determination out-paced their talent, but if the talent is adequate, having the determination is a must.

Q: Looking forward, what concerns do you have for the profession of concert organist, and what are your causes for greatest hope?
A: One of the unusual aspects of the organ performance field is that almost every performance booking or invitation is controlled by another organist. Much of this is because so much of our market is in churches, where the music staff makes such decisions. But it's true in other venues as well. A college or university able to host a performing organist usually will have an office in charge of such events, but in every case I've experienced those professional presenters let the organ faculty select any organists to be booked—the professional may book theater, jazz, piano, etc. with confidence, but when it comes to organ, the confidence disappears. Even the most secular of concert halls will usually ask the local AGO chapter or a prominent local organist for guidance in booking organists. The result is a kind of organ performance inbreeding wherein the field looks inward on itself rather than trying to find the bigger musical performance experience and audience.

This, to my mind, is both the greatest weakness of the organ performance scene, and at the same time perhaps its greatest hope. As we continue to relax the rigidity of our individual tastes in repertoire, instrument types, and schools of performance; as we grow in regarding each other as colleagues rather than potential competition; as we become more ecumenical in our approach to organ performance; as we increasingly turn minor jealousies into a spirit of collegiality within a threatened field—we, as a community, may stumble onto the key for allowing the organ to become the major performance instrument we all want it to be.

Q: Would you care to speak about your experiences as concert manager of touring choirs?
A: We had a wonderful run of several years touring English choirs, including those of York Minster, Christ Church Oxford, Eton College, St. Paul's Cathedral London, and both Clare College and Trinity College Cambridge. Of course touring a European ensemble with dozens of members is expensive, but we always seemed to find enough motivated presenters to make it work including a number of secular presenters with whom we connected at the big performing arts industry trade shows each January in New York.
Nine-Eleven [9/11] was the mark of the end of that run, however. A fully booked tour in October 2001 was cancelled by the choir because of understandable parental concerns. That was not a surprise, although it was

Appendix 2

significant loss of money for the agency which had been paying salaries to staff for many months to develop the tour.

At that point we also had a fully booked tour in place for 2002. This was cancelled for the same reason, and that was something more of a surprise. We kept on working on the tour for 2003 and finally it too was fully booked. The Precentor of that cathedral then cancelled at nearly the last minute, giving no reason except the impression that he simply did not want to do the necessary organization on his side.

For PTCA it was three strikes and out. We simply could not afford to keep spending the time and money needed to book tours which might or might not actually take place.

One of the joys of that period was meeting and traveling with some of the choir members, and especially observing the great sophistication, education, and discipline of the boy trebles who were a remarkable contrast to what I remember of being that age.

Q: With an increasing number of organs in concert halls throughout America, do you foresee a future in which the organ will be heard more often in concert halls than in churches?
A: Wouldn't that be a surprising eventuality! The growth of good instruments in public halls is wonderful news, but the question assumes a continuing downward trend in good new instruments going into churches, and a lessening interest or ability by churches in offering organ performances. It does seem obvious the way things are trending that many churches increasingly will not be able to afford good pipe instruments, and many church presenters already find it difficult enough to justify and pay for top performers. It's logical enough to assume that over the long term the balance between organ recitals in churches and secular halls will continue to shift somewhat, but I doubt the shift will be too radical.

We need to remember also that the surge in concert hall pipe organs has not boosted organ performance numbers as much as one might assume at first glance. Quite a few conductors, it seems, are apathetic or even hostile to organs as part of orchestral programming. And with money always a factor, many orchestras seem to feel there is no point in paying an organ soloist to come in when the orchestra's keyboard person is available and already on hire. Most new concert hall instruments generate a recital series, but I've seen many of them fizzle after a few years—money again, and lack of sufficient audience support.

This reply probably makes me look negative on the future of public organ performance, but I don't feel it that way. The problems are real and aren't likely to go away, but I see an increase in people and institutions really trying to help this art form survive and thrive.

Appendix 2

Q: How important do you regard performance competitions as the launching pad to a concert career?
A: Winning a competition is certainly very helpful in raising one's profile and name recognition, and if the winner is truly motivated toward establishing a performing career the prize money enables further efforts at profile building.

However, if a judge or two on a given competition panel were to be substituted, the results would probably be different. Therefore, I'd rather say that competitions give us performers who are worthy of being considered as standouts in their generation, but not to say that a given winner was necessarily greatly superior to the other competitors.

I'm on the Board of Directors of the Albert Schweitzer Organ Festival competition in Hartford, so if actions speak more loudly than words, I guess I'm a strong believer in organ performance competitions. But I think the biggest value for the competitors is the experience itself and the impetus toward considering trying to build a performing career—sort of trying on the idea for size, as it were.

The ASOF[H] competition has sent some big stars into the field. Three who I represented were Paul Jacobs, winner of the first Schweitzer competition 19 years ago, Simon Thomas Jacobs a subsequent winner who went on to capture the top prize at the St. Albans competition in England, and Christopher Houlihan, winner of a subsequent season's high school division. Still, among the names we may not remember I'd bet there are lots of competitors who benefited from the exercise in terms of helping to sort out for themselves how to put their organ training to best use, including the ones who ended up deciding that attempting a performance career was not where they wanted to go.

Q: Are the requisite skills to maintain a successful concert career perhaps somehow different from those necessary to start that career?
A: It's tempting to say "Yes," because that seems so logical. However, I think the truth is pretty much that the skills are the same, but a successful concert career just demands getting better at them as the performer progresses.

Name recognition is necessary to at least some extent at the beginning or there can be no beginning. It just keeps growing with a career.

Being a stellar performer is necessary to launch a significant career, as well as to maintain it. Ditto for knowing how to program effectively, how to relate to and entertain an audience, how to remain visible, etc. The skills keep growing and developing during a significant performing career, but the specific seeds were there at the beginning or there would have been no

Appendix 2

career launch. A young organist who puts the audience asleep will not have an audience in due course, while a young organist who excites the audience will just get more exciting with time, performing experience, and musical growth.

Are major performers born with capacities others lack, or are they self-created in terms of these skills? My observation is that it's about half of each.

Q: From your long experience, what is the greatest wisdom which you could share with today's organists and today's concert presenters?

A: Simply to keep at it and to keep one's hand in the game when things are difficult. Much of the time, where there's a will there really is a way. I know of many an organ performance series in churches around the country where the reason for continued viability is simply one individual's determination and willingness to work.

Q: You have represented so many luminary names in our profession. Have you learned from some of them? Have you developed lasting friendships with some of them?

A: Yes and yes. And thank you, John, for being one of those luminaries and one of those friends.

Q: I expect that you must be gratified to know that Charles Miller has succeeded you as president of Phillip Truckenbrod Concert Artists. Might you care to speak about your role in preparing Charles for this seamless transition and your ongoing presence with the agency?

A: Charles was my right hand man for over eight years at PTCA so that's when he learned the ropes. He's also had lots of experience as a presenter of organ performers and as an excellent church musician and organist [himself], so he knows the circumstances most presenters need to deal with. He's been very active in the AGO, including chairing a regional convention and serving as program chairman of a national convention.

I'm assisting him now mostly by answering questions which arise, but I'm also open to being assigned specific projects by him.

John Walker: On behalf of myself, many professional colleagues whom you have represented, countless concert presenters, and innumerable concert attendees, I thank you, Phil, for the enduring professional legacy which you have established for concert organists in the United States. Thank you for your lifelong support of the AGO Mission Statement, "to enrich lives through organ and choral music."

Appendix 2

(This material was published in its original form in the September 2016 issue of *The American Organist* magazine and is reprinted by permission of the American Guild of Organists. Words bracketed [thusly] were added herein for greater clarity but were not part of the TAO article.)

Appendix 3: PTCA Roster and Staff

ARTISTS AND ENSEMBLES REPRESENTED FOR VARIOUS PERIODS BETWEEN OCTOBER 1967 AND SEPTEMBER 2015:

ORGANISTS, REGULAR ROSTER, (with commentary)

Archer, Malcolm: at agency transition retired from Winchester College; England, formerly St. Paul's Cathedral, London

Beck, Janice: at agency transition retired; American, Michigan

Biggers, Jonathan: at agency transition deceased, Binghamton University, New York

Björnsson, Ragnar: at agency transition deceased, Iceland

Bowman, David: at agency transition deceased, formerly Alabama State University

Briggs, David: at agency transition living in New York City, formerly Gloucester Cathedral, England

Bruce-Payne, David: at agency transition unknown, sub-organist Westminster Abbey, London

Caire, Patrice: at agency transition deceased; auditorium Maurice Ravel, Lyon, France

Chenault Duo, organists Elizabeth and Raymond: at agency transition retired from All Saints Church, Atlanta, but still actively performing

Clark, Robert: at agency transition retired from Arizona State University, formerly University of Michigan, Ann Arbor, now deceased

Conte, Peter Richard: at agency transition Wanamaker organist, Lord & Taylor (later Macy's) department store, Philadelphia

Corzine, Michael: at agency transition retired, Florida State University, winner National Organ Playing Competition Fort Wayne IN

Danby, Nicholas: at agency transition deceased, England

Davis, Lynne: at agency transition Wichita State University, Kansas, formerly professor of organ at French state universities, winner St. Albans International Organ Competition, England

Daveluy, Raymond: at agency transition retired from St. Joseph's Oratory, Montreal QUE, now deceased

Demers, Isabelle: at agency transition, Baylor University, Waco TX

Appendix 3

Driskill-Smith, Clive: at agency transition All Saints' Episcopal Church, Fort Worth TX, formerly Oxford University, England, Calgary International Organ Competition 2002

Enlow, David: at agency transition Church of the Resurrection, New York City, ASOFH winner

Eschbach, Jesse: at agency transition University of North Texas, Denton

Farr, Stephen: at agency transition unknown, Winchester Cathedral, England, later Corpus Christi College, Cambridge

Filsell, Jeremy: at agency transition Washington DC, formerly England, now St. Thomas Church, Fifth Avenue, New York City

Gary, Roberta: at agency transition retired from University of Cincinnati Conservatory of Music faculty

Gil, Jean-Louis: at agency transition deceased, France

Gillock, Jon: at agency transition living in France, American, specialist in the music of Messiaen

Glasgow, Robert: at agency transition deceased, University of Michigan, Ann Arbor

Guillou, Jean: at agency transition retired, now deceased, France

Hamilton, Stephen: at agency transition retired from Holy Trinity (Episcopal) Church, NYC, American, Minnesota

Harbach (George), Barbara: at agency transition unknown, American

Haas, Douglas: at agency transition retired, Canadian

Herrick, Christopher: at agency transition retired as a freelance performer, England

Heschke, Richard: at agency transition retired from Concordia University, Bronxville NY, now deceased (a member of our original roster)

Hey, Michael: at agency transition Associate Director of Music and Organist at St. Patrick's Cathedral, New York City

Hilse, Walter: at agency transition unknown, Columbia University, New York City

Houlihan, Christopher: at agency transition freelance performer, future College Organist and professor, Trinity College, Hartford, ASOFH winner

Hull, Bradley: at agency transition deceased (a member of our original roster)

Humer, August: at agency transition deceased, Bruckner Conservatory, Linz, Austria

Jacobs, Paul: at agency transition The Juilliard School, New York City, ASOFH winner

Jaquet (Langlais), Marie-Louise: at agency transition retired, France

Jean, Martin: at agency transition Yale University Institute of Sacred Music

Karosi, Balint: at agency transition St. Peter's Lutheran Church, NYC

Koito, Kei: at agency transition unknown, Japan transitioned to Switzerland

Appendix 3

Kynaston, Nicolas: at agency transition retired from Westminster Cathedral, London
Lawrence, Douglas: at agency transition unknown, Melbourne University, Australia
Landis, Kenneth & Ellen: at agency transition unknown, duo-organists, Harrisburg, Pennsylvania. After some years in Massachusetts, Ellen returned to Harrisburg and retired with the honorific Minister of Music Emerita of Market Square Presbyterian Church.
Leguay, Jean-Pierre: at agency transition retired from Notre Dame Cathedral, Paris
Lewis, Huw: at agency transition Hope College, Holland, Michigan, winner National Organ Playing Competition Fort Wayne IN
Lumsden, Andrew: at agency transition Winchester Cathedral, England, formerly sub-organist Westminster Abbey, London
Mantoux, Christophe: at agency transition Saint-Severin, Paris, formerly Chartres Cathedral
Mardirosian, Haig: at agency transition retired from University of Tampa, FL, formerly The American University, Washington DC
McPhee, George: at agency transition Paisley Abbey, Scotland
Mooney, Frederick: at agency transition unknown, Anglican Cathedral, Quebec City, Canada
Mulbury, David: at agency transition unknown, University of Cincinnati, winner AGO National Organ Performance Competition
Murray, Michael: at agency transition church organist in Columbus, Ohio, Telarc Records. Now retired after 31 years as Organist of St. Mark's Episcopal Church in Columbus.
Neswick, Bruce: at agency transition Trinity Episcopal Cathedral, Portland OR, previously St. Philip's Episcopal Cathedral, Atlanta, and Cathedral of St. John the Divine, New York City
Nosetti, Massimo: at agency transition deceased, Turin Cathedral, Italy
O'Donnell, James: at agency transition unknown, Westminster Cathedral, London (tour scheduled but cancelled before executed)
Pardee, Katharine: at agency transition living in England, formerly Syracuse University
Parker-Smith, Jane: England, now deceased
Pierre, Odile: at agency transition unknown, Church of the Madeleine, Paris, now deceased
Pincemaille, Pierre: at agency transition retired, Cathedral of Saint-Denis, France, now deceased
Potts, Nigel: at agency transition Grace Church Cathedral, Charleston SC
Preston, Mary: at agency transition Dallas Symphony Orchestra organist, now retired

Appendix 3

Ramirez, Raul Prieto: at agency transition Ball State University, Ohio, now San Diego CA Civic Organist, Spain relocated to U.S.A.

Ritchie, J. Marcus: at agency transition deceased, St. Philip's Episcopal Cathedral, Atlanta

Robin, Jean-Baptiste: at agency transition Versailles Palace, France

Roubos, Robert: at agency transition unknown, State University of New York, Cortland

Robinson, Lawrence: at agency transition unknown, Virginia Commonwealth University

Robinson, McNeil: at agency transition retired from Park Avenue Christian Church NYC, Manhattan School of Music NYC, now deceased

Rose, Barry: at agency transition unknown, Guildford Cathedral, England

Rose, John: at agency transition College Organist and professor Trinity College, Hartford CT, formerly Cathedral of the Sacred Heart, Newark

Scott, John: at agency transition deceased, St. Thomas Church, Fifth Avenue, NYC, formerly St. Paul's Cathedral, London

Serafin, Jozef: at agency transition unknown, International Nuremberg Organ Competition 1972, Poland

Smith, Larry: at agency transition unknown, Indiana University, now retired

Speller, Frank: at agency transition retired from University of Texas, Austin, now deceased

Spillman, Herndon: at agency transition Louisiana State University, Baton Rouge, now retired

Stender, Ernst-Erich: at agency transition unknown, Germany

Stowe, John Chappell: at agency transition unknown, University of Wisconsin, Madison

Sullivan, Daniel: at agency transition not performing, American

Swartz, Samuel John: at agency transition deceased, American, California

Titterington, David: at agency transition director of St. Albans Festival and competition, England

Twynham, Robert: at agency transition deceased; Cathedral of Mary Our Queen, Baltimore, Maryland

Vernet, Oliver: Monaco Cathedral

Vincent, Robert: at agency transition unknown, Church of St. Martin-in-the-Fields, Trafalgar Square, London; now deceased

Walker, John: at agency transition national president American Guild of Organists and Peabody Conservatory of Music, Baltimore, formerly The Riverside Church NYC and Shadyside Presbyterian Church, Pittsburgh

Watts, Jane: at agency transition unknown, England

Webb, Marianne: at agency transition deceased, Southern Illinois University

Appendix 3

Weir, Gillian: at agency transition retired as a performer, New Zealand relocated to England
Whitehead, William: at agency transition unknown, Trinity College of Music, London
Whiteley, John Scott: at agency transition unknown, assistant organist York Minster, England
Williams, Carol: at agency transition in Lynchburg VA, Wales
(Other organists represented not as individual artists but as members of instrumental duos or ensembles: John Binsfeld, USA; Rupert Gough, England; William O'Meara, Canada.)

My Comments: This is a long list, even considering it covers half a century of agency work. That, in turn, tells us a lot about the organ performance scene of the second half of the 20th century and into the 21st century in this country.

A) It illustrates the widespread conviction by organists of any degree of talent that they belonged in the ranks of concert performers, even if their biggest aptitude was really service playing or academic work. Every working organist has his own platform (instrument) upon which to perform, so none were prevented from performing whether anyone was willing to pay them to do it or not. It also illustrates the *need* organists, like members of any other profession, have to rise in the ranks of their profession. Academics must "publish or perish" we're assured. If one was an organist, that translated, at least partially, to "perform or remain in obscurity." To acquire a professional booking agent was widely seen as one of the credentials which constituted being a "concert organist" instead of being just an "organist," so everyone who fancied himself a performer worked hard to get an agent.

B) It bolsters my memory that there really was a great deal of talent in our organist ranks during that period. Neither we, nor any other agent, added a name to its roster unless the agent felt the person embodied serious talent. The supply/demand ratio always suggested too many good organists and too few serious agents, and certainly too few fee-paying opportunities to perform.

C) It also illustrates the plight of a young emerging agency when faced with a long established agency of commanding reputation as its primary business competition, even if the two agents involved were essentially the same age and had essentially the same amount of experience in the field. The agency with the non-established name (PTCA) had no choice but to be as flexible as possible, and to be open to many of the uncounted performers who approached it seeking representation. Many times these performers just did not click with the market, got discouraged, and dropped out of the

Appendix 3

performing picture; but there were always lots of would-be replacements clamoring at the door. As time went on, our agency grew in stature and reputation, and we, of necessity, became much more exclusive in admitting new performers to our roster—very much like a plastic artist who accepts any reasonable commission at the beginning of a career and then gets progressively more selective as the years add to the artist's stature and reputation.

It was never difficult to find candidates for roster membership—performers and would-be performers kept banging at the door. The difficulty was to select from those candidates the ones who would be the most attractive to presenters and to audiences, and at the same time, those who despite great ambition would be reasonable about the limitations of the market which an agent could not alter.

Often the candidates who presented themselves were just at the raw beginnings of a performance career, and the agent had to essentially guess whether the organist would develop the necessary star power. Sometimes that worked, and sometimes it didn't.

On rare occasions a candidate would surface who already had significant name recognition and credentials as a performer. It might seem that such occasions were a gift from the gods, but in truth the agent's decision in these cases was usually just as difficult if not more so than with the raw beginners who exhibited little more than potential.

One candidate who presented himself to me rather persistently over a fairly long period had a name which would have been recognized by the whole field. He had a large discography on one of the biggest commercial labels in the country and at one point had been represented by one of the large New York agencies for musical performers. So, why not just snap up such a candidate? I saw at least three problems. A) Why had his performance career not flourished when everything seemed to be falling into place so brilliantly? B) Would his well-documented commitment to one side of the great organists' debate between the early music purists and the more 'catholic' oriented organ scene pose problems, and was his side of the equation already over-represented in the market? C) After a major recording label and a New York agent, would he ever really be content with what I felt the market realistically could offer him and would he be content with what I felt we could do for him within those limitations?

No agent wants to add a malcontent to the roster. So I decided the gamble was not worth taking in this case. There is no way to ever know whether that was the best decision, just as there is no way to know if some of my decisions on the potential of younger performers we did not accept were well grounded. One was hopefully getting increasingly better at making educated guesses about roster candidates, but it was never science—it was always, and inevitably, an instinct. As with so many human endeavors, success was mostly a matter of making more good guesses and choices than unfortunate ones.

ORGANISTS, REGULAR ROSTER BY VIRTUE OF ABSORPTION OF HOWARD ROSS AGENCY, (with commentary)

Anderson, Robert: at agency transition deceased, formerly Southern Methodist University, Dallas
Christie, James David: at agency transition Oberlin College OH and Holy Cross College MA, now retired
Obetz, John: at agency transition deceased, RLDS Auditorium, Independence MO
Terry, Carole: at agency transition University of Washington, Seattle, now retired

My comment: I don't recall specifically why Buddy Ross wanted to leave his agency after about nine years of work in the field, but I do recall that his reason for getting into it in the first place was to assist his own primary teacher, Robert Anderson, who for some unremembered reason had dropped off the McFarlane roster (I've heard Karen complain that the Ross business was the agency which existed for just one client). PTCA was still quite young, and these artists had some significant standing, so it was a logical move for me to accept them. It also let Buddy exit the business without feeling he had betrayed his performers.

I think this was the only time we inherited a whole agency (there were subsequent opportunities which we passed over), but throughout my career there were refugees from other agencies seeking roster membership with us, as well as a few who felt they could improve their status by moving from our roster to that of some other agency. There was always some fluidity in roster membership as performers confronted the harsh realities of the performance business and tried to better their status—besides, being human, performers tended to think that any difficulties were the fault of the agent, while of course any success was due to their own talent and charm. Also on the human front, the grass was always greener in the next pasture over. Thus, many in the field were playing a mini-game of musical chairs or at least had an eye open in case they saw a good opportunity to jump into that game.

Appendix 3

ORGANISTS, ROSTER MEMBERSHIP BY VIRTUE OF COMPETITION WIN AGREEMENT, (with commentary)

Aoki, Saki: Chartres winner 2008
Baskeyfield, David: St. Albans Competition 2011, England
Curlee, Matt: at agency transition unknown, winner Chartres Competition 1996, later faculty Eastman School of Music, University of Rochester NY
Dewar, Andrew: at time of agency transition at the 'American Cathedral' in Paris, England, St. Alban's Competition winner
Diaz, James Christopher: at agency transition unknown, winner Dallas International Competition, and winner Calgary Competition
Emmert, Heidi: at agency transition unknown, Germany, winner Chartres, Mendelssohn, Munich, Nuremberg competitions
Foster, Stewart Wayne: at agency transition retired from performing, Florida, winner Dallas International Competition 1997
Hiroe-Lang, Rie: at agency transition unknown, winner Chartres 1998
Hocde, Emmanuel: at agency transition unknown, winner Chartres 2002
Hurd, David: at agency transition General Theological Seminary, New York City, future St. Mary the Virgin Church, NYC, International Congress of Organists (Philadelphia) winner in both performance and improvisation (1977)
Jacobs, Simon Thomas: at agency transition in process of becoming an airline pilot, England, winner of both ASOFH and St. Albans competitions
Jordaan, Herman: at agency transition unknown, St. Albans winner, South Africa
Le Prado, Erwan: at agency transition in Caen, France, winner Chartres Competition
Sheen, Benjamin: at agency transition associate at St. Thomas Church, Fifth Avenue, NYC, England, Longwood winner 2013, future organist of Christ Church Cathedral, Oxford
Shin, Dong-Ill: at agency transition in South Korea, Chartres winner 2006, Korea
Walther, Ulrich: at agency transition unknown, Germany, St. Albans winner
Welch, Bradley Hunter: at agency transition Preston Hollow Presbyterian Church, Dallas, winner Dallas International Organ Competition 2003, future Organist of the Dallas Symphony
Unger, Johannes: at agency transition unknown, winner of St. Albans Competition 2001, Germany
Volostnov, Konstantin, , winner St. Albans Competition 2009, Russia

Appendix 3

My comment: These names come from the winners of organ performance competitions for which we had agreed to add the top winner to our artists' roster for the period until a successor winner was named. Therefore some of these performers were with us only a couple of years by design. Both PTCA and McFarlane had agreements with major competitions to represent their winners. Occasionally both agencies would move a winner over to its regular roster when the successor winner was named, so there was a certain haziness on the provenance of our roster names. PTCA usually promoted these organists under the banner "Winners Circle" to distinguish them from our regular roster.

Looking back at all of the organists we've worked with (and for) I'm struck by how many have died along the way. Perhaps that sounds almost to be a stupid comment; organists are just as much part of the human condition as any other group. But I remember them all as vital people, often at the peak of their contributing years. And even if they had all survived, few of them would be truly ancient even as I write about them here. So all the more reason to set these words on paper, or to launch them into cyber space. These were all people who made a contribution to the art of the organ, and they all deserve to be remembered and mentioned even if just quickly and in passing.

When the winners were foreign nationals, the agency had to apply for a legal entry visa in order for them to perform here as I've noted earlier. This was always an agony because the government agents who controlled the process usually had no idea what an "organist" was, and the regulations specified that persons entering on these visas were to be accomplished artists and recognized in their fields. The agents apparently used pop-culture standards to judge whether the performer was sufficiently famous or not, and that created obvious difficulties for an organist who was young and whose first real brush with public recognition had been winning the competition in question—a competition of which the government agents would be totally ignorant. These problems continue for agents, and are probably becoming even more difficult to navigate. Charles Miller recently asked me for advice on working with the St. Albans' Competition and cited his experience with a recent winner who could not perform engagements booked for him in this country "because USCIS would not approve his visa, citing that he was not a top-level international star and did not have Emmys or Grammys or any international credentials." The agent is left trying to figure out how to build international credentials when the performer is not allowed to cross an international border to perform and thus to build his reputation.

Appendix 3

NON-ORGANIST OR ORGAN-DUO ARTISTS, (with commentary)

Affabre Concinui (male vocal ensemble, Poland)
Amarcord (male a cappella vocal ensemble, Leipzig, Germany)
Alexeyev, Anya (pianist, Russia)
Anthony & Beard (trumpet/organ duo, American; Ryan Anthony now deceased)
Arioso (harp & flute duo)
Avatar Brass (quintet, American)
Banister, Bruce (classical guitar, Germany)
Bells in Motion (hand-bell ensemble, American)
Bernard, Andre (trumpet, France) and Poirier, Rejean (organ, Canada); previously duo with Gil, Jean-Louis (organ, France)
Bisaccia, Paul (American pianist)
Boston Brass (American quintet)
Brown, Thomas (American pianist)
Burley, Raymond (classical guitar, England)
Canterbury Cathedral, Choir of (men and boys, England)
Chanson (male vocal septet, American)
Chapelle du Roi (vocal ensemble, England)
Christ Church Choir of (men and boys, Oxford, England)
Clare College, Choir of (mixed voices, Cambridge, England)
Conti, Mirian (American pianist)
Chrysolith (harp & flute duo): Rebecca Flannery, harp, and Diane Kern, flute
Cutmore, Jason (American pianist)
DeChiaro, Giovanni (classical guitar, American)
Dilzell, Frederick (classical guitar, American)
Duo Solisti (Kathleen Scheide organ & Zofie Vokalkova flute)
English Guitar Duo (Raymond Burley and Arne Brattland)
Eton College Choir (men and boys, England)
Fanfare Consort (early music sextet, American)
Filsell/Lewis Duo (Jeremy Filsell, organ, and Oliver Lewis, violin, England)
Fletcher, Peter (classical guitar, American)
Flippin, Thomas (classical guitar, American)
Gloucester Cathedral Choir (men & boys, England)
Gough Duo, violin and organ, England, at agency transition not working as a duo, Rupert Gough at St. Bartholomew the Great, West Smithfield, London
Gramley, Joseph (American percussionist)

Appendix 3

Gypsy Moods, accordion and violin
Harp & Organ (harpist Kathleen Bride & organist Jon Gillock)
Heindel, Kim (American harpsichord, lautenwerk)
Himy, Eric (American pianist)
Impressions (American dancer Timothy Martin & American pianist Thomas Brown)
Inman Piano Trio (American)
Jones, Ieuan (harpist, Wales)
Jones, Michael Leighton, English baritone, with organist David Bruce-Payne
Konevets Quartet (male a cappella ensemble, St. Petersburg, Russia)
Laughton & O'Meara (trumpet & organ, Canada)
Loman, Judy (harp, American)
Liber unUsualis (Medieval vocal ensemble, American)
Linden Duo, The (Kimberly McCaul Risinger flute and Angelo L. Favis classical guitar)
Luminosity (Joanna Goldstein flute and Sarah Stuart harp, American)
Mazaika (accordion and violin, France)
Moscow Nights (string trio, Russia)
Muro, Don (electronic music, American)
New College, Choir of (men and boys, Oxford, England) scheduled tour did not take place
New England Spiritual Ensemble (later National Spiritual Ensemble, American)
New Pro-Arte Guitar Trio (England)
Novacek/Bissiri (classical Guitar Duo)
Nutmeg Brass Quintet
Organized Rhythm (organ-percussion duo): Clive Driskill-Smith and Joseph Gramley
Onyx Brass (quintet, England)
Paulsson and Huff (tenor saxophone and organ): Anders Paulsson, Sweden, and Harry Huff, New York City; later Paulssen & Canning
Petricic, Marko (bayan accordionist, American)
Presidio Saxophone Quartet (American)
Rastrelli Cello Quartet (Russia)
Recorder Trio Cologne (Germany)
Rejoicensemble (American Gospel sextet)
Richner, Thomas (pianist): at agency transition deceased, organist "The Mother Church" of Christian Science, Boston, Rutgers University, NJ; also
Richner-Rose Duo with organist John Rose
Rittenhouse Organ and Brass Ensemble, The (Philadelphia, John Binsfeld, organist)

Appendix 3

Rodolfus Choir, The (chamber choir, England)
Rodrigo Guitar Trio (England)
Rose Ensemble (vocal, American)
Schliessmann, Burkard (pianist, Germany)
Shelley-Egler Duo (flutist Frances Shelly, Wichita State University KS, organist Steven Egler, Central Michigan University)
Simply Gershwin (American duo John Whitley, tenor, and Paul Bisaccia, piano)
Smith, Robert Edward (harpsichordist): at agency transition a composer living in Boston MA
Smoky Mountain Brass (American brass orchestra)
St. Albans Abbey, Choir of (men and boys, England)
St. George's Chapel, Windsor Castle, Choir of (men and boys, England)
St. Paul's Cathedral, Choir of (men and boys, London)
Steinbach & Helvey (piano duo, American)
Stringer, Vincent Dion (American bass-baritone)
Texas Boys Choir, The
Tin Pan Alley Alive (vocalist David Giardina and pianist Paul Bisaccia, American)
Trinity College, Choir of (mixed voices, Cambridge, England)
Trio Sonata (flute, oboe, guitar; American)
True North Brass (quintet, Canada)
Trumpet & Organ (Edward Tarr, trumpet, and Irmtraud Kruger, organ)
Vento Chiaro (Woodwind quintet, American)
Vienna Vocal Consort (Austria)
Virtuosi Quintet, The (woodwinds)
Von Trapp, Elisabeth (soprano/guitarist, American)
Wells Cathedral Choir of (men and boys, England)
Williamson, Malcolm (composer and performer): at agency transition deceased; Master of the Queen's Music to HM Elizabeth II
Yankele (Klezmer ensemble, Russia/England)
Yanofitsky, Mikail (Russian pianist)
York Minster, Choir of (men and boys, England)

My comment: As I compiled this list I was surprised by how many names showed up here. As you may have guessed, a number of these launches were not very successful as we constantly tried to break into a wider performance market, while on the other hand several of them became recognizable names on the performance scene and enjoyed rewarding success. This was especially true of some ensembles, the New England Spiritual Ensemble and ensemble Amarcord being good examples of groups which approached us with no profile in the American performance

Appendix 3

market but who then in short order claimed genuine success. The European choirs for the most part already had high name recognition here because of their famous host institutions.

At the point we started to branch into a second roster (of non-organists) we were in a far worse competitive stance vis-a-vis older agencies than was even the case when Karen McFarlane took over from Lillian Murtagh. Essentially, we were crawling out very far on a big limb. We did experience some success in becoming a 'general' agency for musical performers, although I think it was never our primary goal; it was mostly just wanting to add some frosting to the economic cake. Organists remained our primary focus and identity.

STAFF MEMBERS OF PHILLIP TRUCKENBROD CONCERT ARTISTS BETWEEN 1967 AND 2015, (with commentary)

Raymond Albright (still in the organ business, now building consoles at Austin Organs in Hartford). Ray was my technology right hand and savior for about the last two-thirds of my time with the agency. He filled in my vast ignorance of anything technical and insured that PTCA kept pace with every new development as it came along. And he rescues me still, no longer as a business partner but now as a friend. However you are reading this, as an e-book or on paper, you would not be doing so were it not for Ray's continued toleration of my technological ignorance and his valued friendship.

Michael W. Anderson
Mark J. Arend
Kenneth J. Bartschi (now a practicing attorney in Hartford and himself an organist)
Gary Bibens (now Director of Music & Arts, Crozet United Methodist Church, Waynesboro, Virginia, a choral musician but not an organist)
Thomas Bohlert (himself an organist, retired from East Hampton Presbyterian Church, Long Island, New York)
Victoria Burns
Stacy Cahoon

Appendix 3

Scott Christiansen (himself an organist)
Jennifer J. Colman
Stephen Z. Cook (himself an organist with an earned doctorate, currently at Trinity Episcopal Church, Portsmouth, Virginia)
Christopher Corbett
Erik Eickhoff (himself an organist, currently a staff member at AGO national headquarters in New York City; my last staff assistant)
Donald Funk (himself an organist, now at West Avon Congregational Church, Connecticut)
John P. Higgins (himself an organist, now at St. Patrick Church, East Hampton, Connecticut)
Nate Howe
Michael Kearney
Vaughn Mauren (himself an organist, now Artistic Director of ASOFH)
Charles A. Miller (now president of PTCA as my successor and himself an organist; also Director of Music at Cherry Hill Presbyterian Church, Dearborn, Michigan)
John Albert Moseley
James Rodgers (now deceased; himself an organist)
Jane Wozniak (my first staff assistant)
Tradd (A foundling dog who accompanied me to the office faithfully for years and kept us all entertained, although I'm not sure that he ever cared very much about the future of the organ as a performance instrument. He did care, however, about our delivery man who would stop at a butcher shop to pick up a nice bone for Traddie on his way to our office. Other than on anticipated delivery days, he would sleep at my feet as I typed data into our computer. Tradd was essentially the agency mascot for several years and if I'd had my head screwed on correctly I would have (should have) used him in our general promotional efforts to lend the humanizing touch that only an animal can lend to a human endeavor. He certainly would have added more charm than did my photo, which is probably why my photo was used extremely rarely. Tradd died while in agency service at an unknown age. He was not the only staff member whose loss was regretted along the way, but he is the only one for whom I shed actual tears for several days.)

My comment: It took some time to be able to compile an accurate and complete list of former staff members, but I'd waited over four years since retirement to find the energy and interest to try to reconstruct such a list, or to write even the first word in attempting to tell the agency's story (I needed at that point to clear my head for the sake of perspective as much as to remember for the sake of accuracy), and many of these people had worked with us some decades ago by then. Also, naturally, there was enough turnover that some of these people were not with us for long periods as they sought to move from entry level jobs to better pay and greater responsibility. The best were with us for a collective several decades, while others dropped in for cameo visits of a few months or a couple of years. All were instrumental in our long-term success, however, and to all I acknowledge indebtedness and express deep gratitude.

In addition to paid vacation time after one year of service, we gave our staff two other paid mini-breaks: most of, or at least the last few days of Holy Week, and then the gap between Christmas Eve and January 2. These were essentially dead zones for our work because most of our presenters were church musicians who did not surface outside of church during those periods. I frequently worked anyway, catching up on this or that, although if the weather was nice enough by Holy Week I would sneak in some gardening time. Essentially we just closed the office during these periods, and judging from our phone message machines, no one noticed.

AGO & RELATED CONVENTIONS TREATED AS TRADE SHOWS (with commentary)
(City/Organization/Convention Type: N=national; R=regional; ICO=International Congress of Organists; MWC=Mid-Winter Conclave; Number of conventions)

Albany NY: AGO,R,1
Atlanta GA: AGO,N,1
Binghamton NY: AGO,R,1
Boston MA: AAM, 1/AGO,N,2/New England Presenters,1 (total 4)
Cambridge UK: AGO,ICO,1
Cape Cod MA: AGO,R,1
Chicago IL: AGO,N,1 & R,1 (total 2)
Dallas TX: AGO,N,2
Denver CO: AGO,N,1
Des Moines IA: AGO,R,1
Detroit MI: AGO,N,1
Evanston IL: AGO,R,1
Hartford CT: AGO,R,2/AAM,N,1/New England Presenters,1 (total 4)

Appendix 3

Houston TX: AGO,N,2
Long Island NY: AGO,R,1
Los Angeles CA: AGO,N,1
Minneapolis MN: AGO,N,2
Nashville TN: AGO,N,1
Newark NJ: AGO,R,1
New Haven CT: AGO,R,1
Newport RI: AGO,R,1
New York NY: AGO,N,1/AAM,N,1/ALCM,N,1/CMA,N,1/ISAP,N,2/APAP,N,7 (total 13)
Philadelphia PA: AGO,N,1,R,1/AGO,ICO,1 (total 3)
Pittsfield MA: AGO,R,1
Providence RI: AGO,R,1
San Diego CA: AGO R,1
San Francisco CA: AGO,N,1
Seattle WA: AGO,N,2
St. Louis MO: AGO,MWC,1
Springfield MA: AGO,R,1
Washington DC: AGO,N,2
Westchester County NY: AGO,R,1 (1970 first AGO booth mounted)
West Palm Beach FL: AAM,N,1
Wilmington DE: AGO,R,1
Winooski/Burlington VT: AGO,R,1
Worcester MA: AGO,R,1

My Comment: Utilizing AGO conventions, which we had to attend anyway, as "trade shows" by mounting exhibition space seemed an obvious idea to me, and I was always a bit surprised that McFarlane did not join us in that approach. But that may have been due to a personality difference more than anything else—Karen relied on circulating and chatting, at which she had a natural talent, and I had always loved trade shows since my parents let me go with them to a Home Show exhibition in Des Moines while I was still a small school boy.

Anyway, for me it was the exhibition aspect which provided much of the fun of attending these ubiquitous conventions. The extent to which our booths helped promote our artists is impossible to know but would be fun to know in retrospect. I'm sure they did help to some degree. They were another form of advertising and we needed to exploit every angle possible for the endless job of creating and increasing artist name recognition and standing.

One of the fascinating things I discovered about human nature through this process was that people seem to instinctively shy away from a booth which is manned unless they have a specific reason to talk with the agent. For the merely curious, the fear of having to talk with a booth-tender appeared to be a negative. I learned to occasionally leave the booth and stand at the end of the aisle watching the traffic. Then, with the booth empty of a tender, lots of people would approach and sort through the various promotional papers and items we had on display—often the very same people who had been casing the booth earlier but apparently did not want to be engaged by an agent who had 'something to sell.'

I had always loved trade shows and was enamored of the give-away promotional items companies utilized at them. Fewer booths than I would have expected had such items to hand out at AGO conventions, which may have testified to the slim financial margins which exhibitors had to contend with. But I felt it was important for people to be able to walk away with something tangible from our booth, so we added the cost of such promo items to the already large investment that AGO conventions called for. Sometimes the give-away items were as substantial as compact disc recordings, and sometimes as stereotypical as writing pens with the agency name inscribed on them. Whether such investments made sense on a tight budget, or made any difference in our marketing, I'm not sure. But at least they helped me justify our effort at these conventions, which I resolutely insisted had to have a trade-show component for PTCA.

Appendix 4: Stephen Z. Cook Remembering His Work at PTCA

I worked in the office at PTCA in West Hartford, Connecticut, from January 2002 to July 2005, and then on and off part-time remotely from 2006-2010, and then as an unsolicited sounding board for various artists and presenters after that. I learned very quickly at PTCA that in order to do business with people—artists and presenters, the workload goes a little bit easier if you make friends with them (and they make friends with you).

John Scott was one of these people with whom I made friends. Phil took me to the St. Alban's competition in July 2003. On a side trip to London I met John at high tea, thanks to Phil and his desire to meet with all of his artists whenever geographically possible. I later had the privilege of turning pages for John a few times when he was on tour in the United States. When he became the Director of Music at St. Thomas in New York he asked if I would want to play one of the Sunday afternoon recitals, so I eventually did. My last conversation with John took place about a year after he left the agency; a simple catching up on life sort-of exchange. That he always remembered to thank me, the underling in the office, for my work on his behalf, and then stayed in touch really meant a lot to me, and especially so upon his untimely death.

When I started working at the agency, George W. Bush was President of the United States and a little more than a year after the terrorist attacks on September 11, 2001 he created the cabinet-level Office of Homeland Security. Customs and immigration fell under this department, and it was part of my job at the agency to fill out in detail the various visa application forms for the artists who lived outside of the United States, abiding by the new rules in a post-9/11 world. I quickly realized this unseen and daunting work to be crucial to the agency's success. If the artist couldn't cross the border and work, the agency made no money.

Having had no education or experience in this field, I was extremely grateful for the trail of paperwork Charles Miller left behind for his successor to study, which I devoured so I would never be responsible for a failed tour. It was a stressful process, akin to tax form 1040 on which you don't take the standard deduction and [instead] itemize everything.

The application process went like this: The Department of Homeland Security required that all applications for the O, P1, and P1s visas include union letters [of support] (AGO, AFM, etc.), fully executed signed contracts, a mountain of evidence of the performer's accomplishments, and a big whopping check that the agency fronted months in advance of the

Appendix 4

tour. This was the first step towards the artist getting their visa. The second and last step the artist[s] had to do themselves, which involved scheduling a face-to-face meeting at the nearest U.S. Consulate (London, Paris, etc.) and traveling to that location for the meeting and official stamp of approval [in their passports].

The visa applications for the well-known and oft-traveled organists John Scott, Pierre Pincemaille, and the exponentially large Eton College Choir were tremendous work, but were always approved without a hitch. I never worried about them. However, the newer touring performers like organist Clive Driskill-Smith and the Rastrelli String Quartet, always gave me great pause. I close my comments on this subject with an article Phil included in his weekly newsletter from October 2004:

BEHIND THE SCENES: *A Narrow Escape* [from a PTCA newsletter]

If you've ever wondered what the day-to-day work of an agency representing classical musicians could be like, here is just one story from many we could tell which will give you some idea.

A European cello quartet which is currently in the midst of its American debut tour was nearly locked out of the country because of the 9/11 attacks three years ago.

The Rastrelli Cello Quartet, whose members live in Germany but carry Russian passports, needed to fly to the United States on October 6 in order to keep their debut tour engagements. Their entry visas were approved only the day before, October 5, following interviews at the U.S. embassy in Germany. But even that tight schedule was hanging by the thinnest of threads because the official documents of approval, necessary for entering the embassy, had not yet reached us in Hartford to be forwarded to the artists.

The visa application process for the ensemble was begun on schedule six months ago by this agency, the earliest date allowed by visa regulations. After careful monitoring suggested the process was becoming dangerously slow, Stephen Cook of this agency enlisted help from the office of Congressman John Larson of Connecticut. At that point the application had been on the desk of a worker at the Vermont office of the U.S. Citizenship & Immigration Service for four months with no resolution.

Congressman Larson's staff succeeded in getting the application moved to an adjudicator, one step up the ladder. At that point, additional application documentation was asked for and submitted by us. This demand including asking for a letter from a second "peer group;" one more than is required in the process (a "peer group" for performers is usually a union such as the American Federation of Musicians or the American Guild of Musical Artists).

Appendix 4

After additional weeks of requests from the Congressman's office to speed the process, a third set of new application documents was demanded, and submitted by the agency. At this point, the help of United States Senator Christopher Dodd of Connecticut was also enlisted, and the application was bumped up one more step to a Supervisor in Vermont, but still without resolution. More submissions were later called for and submitted.

With one week to go before the quartet had to catch their flight to the U.S. the application had finally reached the equivalent of the supreme court at the visa office in Vermont, but there was no guarantee a decision would be reached in time. Even if it was approved, the visas could not be granted in Germany as regulations specified without the applicants holding the official approval papers, and it was obvious Vermont could not get those to the agency in time by regular mail, the only method used.

As we were trying to line up substitute performers and dreading how to break the news to presenters on the tour, word finally came on October 1 that the application had been approved with just five days to go before the flight to the U.S.

At this point Congressman Larson's office began trying to set up an appointment for the interviews in Germany even though the documents normally required for this process were not yet in hand. The appointment was finally granted on the morning of October 5, and the quartet drove three hours to Frankfurt from their homes in Stuttgart. When the visas were at last attached to their passports, it was less than 24 hours to flight time.

As the quartet was high over the Atlantic on October 6, the official document of approval arrived at our office in Connecticut. The whole process had consumed days of office time to produce four separate application submissions and monitoring of the process without being able to talk directly to anyone in the government bureaucracy which operates the process. Stephen Cook, who handles our visa applications, made five separate trips to Congressman Larson's office during the process, as well as hours phoning and faxing.

Foreign artists have had increasing difficulty gaining entrance visas during the past couple of years, and a number of well-established performers have had to cancel scheduled appearances in the United States as a result.

U.S. authorities have increased their scrutiny of visa applications in general, and approval times have lengthened as a result. Applications for performers cannot be made earlier than six months from the time of the first tour booking, and scrutiny of performers' applications has increased

Appendix 4

greatly since U.S. officials began to fear that terrorist organizations would attempt to use artist's visas to get their operatives into the country legally.

In many cases approval is finally given, but it comes too late for the performers to keep their touring schedule.

The Rastrelli Cello Quartet is currently performing in an American debut tour which will take them to nine cities in seven states plus Canada this month. Its members were trained in Russia, where three of them studied at the famous music conservatory in St. Petersburg and named the quartet after the Italian architect hired to build Peter the Great's capital. Two are also members of the famous Wuertemberg Chamber Orchestra in Germany.

Appendix 5: Kenneth J. Bartschi Recalls His Work with PTCA

In May 1989, I began what would be a four-year stint as Booking Director at Phillip Truckenbrod Concert Artists. I had not envisioned working in arts management when I was an undergraduate student at Potsdam College's Crane School of Music where I was a music education major. Nor did I imagine that my time at PTCA would be a bridge to a career as an appellate lawyer. After Crane, I had gone on to earn a Master of Music degree from Arizona State University in organ performance. PTCA, which at that time concentrated on concert organists and English choirs, included my organ professor, the late Robert Clark on its roster. Bob alerted me to the opportunity at PTCA. Needing a break from school and longing to return to the Northeast, I jumped at the opportunity.

Being an organist myself proved to be quite useful in my work as Booking Director. I could speak the language of the artists and the presenters. Given the custom-made nature of pipe organs and the variety of builders, I knew the difference between a tracker and an electro-pneumatic instrument, what the various stops sounded like, whether the instrument was particularly suited to certain repertoire such as French Romantic or Baroque. All of this was particularly important when suggesting performers for presenters because organists often specialized in particular composers or styles that can be found in several centuries of organ literature.

As for the English choirs, arranging tours required figuring out how long it took to get from point A to point B by [chartered] bus. Often, it meant finding a presenter who could be persuaded to present a concert mid-week, not always an easy task because while the choirs were wonderful, presenting them was quite an undertaking. The presenter had to come up with the funds to pay for it and provide housing. Sometimes it was necessary, or at least desirable, to fill in a geographic gap between concert venues. This task required finding a venue and then persuading the presenter it could work financially and logistically. The presenters put a lot of work into putting on these concerts, but the choirs were just wonderful and the afterglow usually made up for the heavy lifting beforehand.

And then there were the visas. The English choirs and European organists needed H-1 visas. Applying for them required gathering various materials and sending them to an INS office in Vermont. Occasionally, it was necessary to call that office, which was staffed with people who give

Appendix 5

bureaucrats a bad name. I cannot imagine what the process is like now, given the ever-increasing restrictions on visas.

Part of the work included some travel. I remember attending national AGO conventions in Atlanta and Boston and a regional convention in Philadelphia. There were certainly others that have faded from my memory. I would travel parts of the choir tours. Phil also took me to London in the early 1990s. Sometimes travel meant going to New York or Washington to hear a concert and meet and greet afterwards. I'm not one for small talk, but these were my people, so it was easy to converse about the music or the instrument.

I cannot possibly remember all the artists I heard, but they were excellent performers. Some of the names that come to mind include Mary Preston, John Rose, John Walker, McNeil Robinson, Jean-Pierre Leguay, Kei Koito, the late John Scott, and Christopher Herrick. I had the good fortune to hear St. Paul's Cathedral Choir and the Choirs of Trinity College and Clare College Cambridge.

When I moved on to law school and practicing law, I took with me some valuable skills acquired by working at the agency. First, Phil's prior experience as a journalist made him an excellent writer and teacher. Through his gentle editing, I learned how to be persuasive in a subtle fashion, avoiding superlatives and hype while presenting artists in the best light. That skill has served me well in brief writing and stands in contrast to the histrionic writing I see too often in opposing briefs.

Second, while organists are not rock stars, they do have egos, some more tender than others. Dealing with the artists (and those presenters who fancied themselves artists) occasionally required diplomacy, good humor, a thick skin. Honing those skills at PTCA has served me well in [my] career as an appellate lawyer when it comes to dealing with clients, other lawyers, and judges, who, as it turns out, may also have egos.

Another aspect of PTCA that remains with me to this day is that, besides being my first job in the real world, I was able to be openly gay. Today that is fairly unremarkable, but in the late '80s and early '90s, this was no small thing. Being able to be myself at work at that time was truly a gift.

It has been more than a quarter century since I moved on from PTCA. I am glad to know that Charles Miller is continuing the tradition. Choral music, organ music, and chamber music are wonderful art forms, and I am happy that I had a small part in bringing that music to others.

Appendix 6: Charles A. Miller Recalls His Initial Time With PTCA

BOOKING DIRECTOR 1993-2000

My time at the agency started innocently enough as a side job to supplement a three-quarter-time position as director of music and organist at a small, English-style country Episcopal Church in the quaint village of Tariffville, Connecticut. This all came about because during my senior year at University of Michigan I was in a long-distance relationship with Raymond Albright, one of the owners of the company under which the agency operated. I decided upon my graduation that this Midwest boy needed to move east. During the first few months of my new agency job, I recall doing routine things like filing, double checking concert calendars, getting to know the database, and stuffing and licking endless promotional mailing envelopes that Phil would put together – well before the advent of e-mail. This seemingly mindless work, though, exposed me to the bios and fliers of the artists the agency represented and of their repertoire and bookings. My colleague, booking director Ken Bartschi, allowed me as able to sit in on his phone calls and watch as he put promotional letters and contracts together, so I would get to know the ropes if he ever needed to be absent. And I got the sense that even early on I was being not-so-covertly groomed to someday have a bigger role in the agency.

After about a years' time, Ken Bartschi decided to go back to school to become a lawyer, and this left the position of booking director open. And so, at age 26, with only one year of experience in the artist management field, Phil asked me to take this position – an honor to be sure. It was pretty heady stuff for a recent college graduate. Now it was me in the driver's seat, launched into filling recital tours for prominent European artists (Christopher Herrick, Nicolas Kynaston, John Scott, and John Scott Whitely, England; Jean-Pierre Leguay, France; Kei Koito, Switzerland; and many

Charles (seated) and Phil comparing notes.

others) and also dealing with the endless and complicated paperwork for the visa applications (and [charter] bus reservations, and home-stay arrangements for the singers, etc.) necessary to get the English cathedral and university choirs into the U.S. for their concert tours. Reams and reams of paper were used up for these visa applications (something, now in 2020, that has gotten even more complicated, stressful, and expensive!). It was also fascinating to observe Phil so expertly do the "dirty work" of the agency: balancing the finances, dealing with the endless advertising, exasperating negotiations with cranky and difficult European cathedral deans and choir school administrators to get choir tours organized, and then dealing with the fallout when [some of] those tours, fully booked by PTCA, were forced to be cancelled by the cathedral deans at the 11th hour.

Still to this day, there are fond remembrances (as a 20-something, impressionable young organist-booking agent) of going to England for the first time to see York Minster and a small vacation in the Yorkshire countryside, hearing the organ of St. Paul's Cathedral, London, and touring and dining in the grand halls of Trinity College, Cambridge; "hanging out" back stage with the always-charming John Scott on choir tours or when he was playing solo recitals; getting a severe second-degree sunburn on my neck and legs sitting outside while Nicholas Kynaston practiced on the outdoor Spreckels Organ at San Diego's Balboa Park; meeting and getting to know some of the luminaries in the organ field at AGO conventions, and having many over to the house for cocktail hour when they performed in Hartford; the day-to-day connections with the artists on the roster, who filled my days with colorful stories and endless laughter.

After seven years, however, the "itch" to devote my life to full-time music making and going back to school became much more of a driving force in my life. In 2000, I left my position as booking director and completed my master's degree in choral conducting. Following graduation, and for the next 13 years, I found myself back in full-time church work in Connecticut and then Washington D.C. and then Albany, New York. Lessons learned and the hundreds of professional connections made during my seven years at the agency did serve me well, and very much continue to do so today.

Of my nearly eight years as booking director, truly the most gratifying aspect of my agency work was simply working with and for the artists on the roster. And this remains true today in my present role as president and owner of the agency – a role graciously entrusted to me by Phil in September 2015 at the time of his retirement. All along, my training as an organist, church musician, aspiring recitalist, and my own presentation of recitals at the churches I served, gave me knowledge of what it took to make organ recitals and choir concerts work well. I also credit my mother

Appendix 6

with providing perhaps via DNA but definitely with educating her children the ability to efficiently organize projects and keep meticulous schedules! With the artists on the roster, I could, much of the time, intuitively anticipate their recital needs before they even knew that they needed things. My mother, a nurse, was a great nurturer and care-giver. This, too, was also imbued into her children. I simply love caring for the artists and making sure that they have everything they need in order to step out on stage and engage in the art of live performance. This also goes for my work with the presenters of these artists. One of the great joys of this job is having really great friends literally from coast to coast and north to south, with whom I share the love of the pipe organ. Some of these presenters have become so loyal that they will always book at least one PTCA concert organist each season, for which I am immensely grateful, and these friendships are renewed with each new concert booking.

In 1967 Phil created an arts agency, and with the incredible assistance and support from John Rose and Raymond Albright, it became one of the powerhouses within the pipe organ field. And the name "Phillip Truckenbrod" remains an indelible and instantly recognized part of the fabric of this field. I remain honored to have been asked to lead the agency into its sixth decade of service to the pipe organ and the incredible musicians who perform upon this heroic instrument!

Appendix 7: A Quotation from Paul Bisaccia's Book "Piano Player: Memoir and Masterclass"

I finally had my first television show broadcast on PBS in May of 1996. Now I needed a manager - but how to go about it? I sent a copy of the TV show to Edward Jablonski, the much esteemed George Gershwin biographer. He wrote back to me on his old Underwood typewriter (which I thought was quaint) telling me how much he loved the show. Then he wrote, when it came to managers, his colleagues in the music business all agreed, "When you've got 'em you don't want 'em, when you want 'em you can't get 'em." His quote, from the lengthy title of that obscure Gershwin song, was not exactly what I wanted to hear. My teacher Luiz also had bad luck with managers. I remained undeterred. I asked Larry Allen Smith, the Dean of the Hartt School, for some advice. He told me he'd put in a word with Phillip Truckenbrod Concert Artists, a much respected management agency with an impressive roster of artists.

    Phillip Truckenbrod came to a concert of mine and signed me up right away. He has been my manager ever since – the only manager I've ever had. He is the exact opposite of what we usually think of as a manager. He is quiet and low key, with a Midwestern politeness. (He's originally from Iowa.) He wrote up a contract that was generous to me beyond anything I have ever seen in the business. He arranged hundreds of successful concerts for me and helped my career reach a new level, putting the prestige of his agency and its finances behind my career. If there is a constant thread running through this book, it is how much the people we surround ourselves with contribute to our success. Phillip is at the top of that list. He also runs a small recording company. Towerhill Recordings was started in the 1960's by Michael Nemo. Tom Richner, a fine pianist, recorded many albums for this company. Phillip revived the company in the mid 1990's and I have recorded 19 CDs under the Towerhill label. As I write these words, Phillip is celebrating the 45th anniversary of Phillip Truckenbrod Concert Artists. What a milestone! It just shows that sometimes the good guys do finish first.

(Reprinted by permission of the author.)

Made in the USA
Middletown, DE
27 December 2020